GOETHE

FAUST

PART ONE

TRANSLATED
BY PHILIP WAYNE

PENGUIN BOOKS
BALTIMORE · MARYLAND

Penguin Books Ltd, Harmondsworth, Middlesex, England
Penguin Books Inc., 3300 Clipper Mill Road, Baltimore 11, Md, U.S.A.
Penguin Books Pty Ltd, Ringwood, Victoria, Australia

—

This translation first published 1949
Reprinted 1951, 1953, 1954, 1956 (twice), 1958,
1960, 1961, 1962, 1963 (twice), 1965 (twice)

—

Copyright © Philip Wayne 1949

—

Made and printed in Great Britain
by Richard Clay (The Chaucer Press), Ltd,
Bungay, Suffolk
Set in Monotype Bembo

—

*Terms for performance or adaptation of 'Faust' in this new translation
may be obtained from the League of Dramatists,
84 Drayton Gardens, S.W.10,
to whom all applications for permission should be made*

This book is sold subject to the condition
that it shall not, by way of trade, be lent,
re-sold, hired out, or otherwise disposed
of without the publisher's consent
in any form of binding or cover
other than that in which
it is published

NNN
3-

THE PENGUIN CLASSICS
FOUNDER EDITOR (1944–64): E. V. RIEU
PRESENT EDITORS:
Betty Radice and Robert Baldick

L 12

CONTENTS
WITH SUMMARY OF SCENES

Goethe – Biographical Note	11
Introduction	13

FAUST · PART ONE

DEDICATION   29

PRELUDE IN THE THEATRE   31

PROLOGUE IN HEAVEN   39

NIGHT · FAUST'S STUDY (i):   43
Faust is disconsolate; he conjures up the Earth Spirit, but without power to detain him. Faust and Wagner, his 'Famulus' or Servitor. **Faust broods again, and desires death. Bells and voices in the Easter Dawn prevent him from taking his life.*

OUTSIDE THE CITY GATE: 57
Various citizens, soldiers; then Faust and Wagner; they meet the mysterious Poodle.

FAUST'S STUDY (ii):   70
Faust, more peaceful, studies St John; but he is disturbed by the Poodle, which assumes a menacing shape; Faust compels Mephistopheles to appear, from the form of the Poodle; he interrogates Mephistopheles who is trapped, but rescued by spirits, who lull Faust to sleep.

FAUST'S STUDY (iii):   82
Mephistopheles returns, and, with full argument, the wager is made.*

Note. The scenes between the two marks * above were added by Goethe many years after his original version; which accounts for the kinder companionship with Wagner and the tone mellowed by experience: in this, and in his wager with Mephisto, Faust's fate is developing in accordance with the wager in the Prologue, between Satan and the Lord God. The beautiful, retrospective 'Dedication' was also added later, as were the 'Prelude' and the 'Prologue' – see Introduction, p. 19.

Contents

[MEPHISTOPHELES AND THE FRESHMAN]	93
[MEPHISTOPHELES AND FAUST SET OUT]	99

AUERBACH'S CELLAR IN LEIPZIG: 100
> Drinking party. Fiery pranks by Mephistopheles: Faust is introduced here to a first degree of worldly grossness. Mephistopheles causes mirage in which the two disappear.

WITCH'S KITCHEN: 110
> Faust is repelled by this second degree of devilment; but he is enraptured with a vision of woman's beauty, and he accepts the rejuvenating potion.

A STREET: 121
> First encounter with Margareta; Faust demands her of Mephistopheles.

EVENING: 123
> Mephistopheles leaves Faust alone in Margareta's room, in her absence. The devil places a casket for her; she returns, and finds the jewels.

A WALK: 128
> Mephistopheles is irate because Margareta's mother has given the jewels to a priest.

NEIGHBOUR'S HOUSE: 130
> Margareta and Martha her neighbour. Mephistopheles tells Martha of the death of her husband and arranges a return with Faust.

A STREET: 136
> Faust gives reluctant consent to the ruse of Mephistopheles.

IN MARTHA'S GARDEN: 138
> Faust's first love-scene with Margareta; Mephistopheles entertains Martha – the famous 'quartet', in and out of the scene.

A SUMMER-HOUSE   144

FOREST AND CAVERN: 145
> Faust, alone, feels a return of purer aspiration, but is tempted back to amorousness by Mephistopheles.

MARGARETA'S ROOM: 150
> Her heart is troubled, and she sings sadly at her wheel.

Contents

MARTHA'S GARDEN: 151
Second love-scene; Margareta questions Faust's beliefs; Mephistopheles scoffs at this, and gloats over the approaching night.

AT THE WELL: 156
A neighbour-girl's gossip strikes appalling fear into the heart of Margareta.

A SHRINE IN THE RAMPARTS: 158
Margareta's remorseful anguish and prayer.

NIGHT: 159
Valentine, Margareta's brother, is heavy-hearted with evil rumour of her; he challenges Faust and Mephistopheles, and is treacherously slain in a duel; dying, he curses his sister.

CATHEDRAL NAVE: 165
Margareta is plagued by an Evil Spirit, and in her remorse she swoons.

WALPURGIS NIGHT: 167
(Presumably this is the May Day Eve a year after the death of Valentine.)
The Festival of Witches and Spirits upon the Brocken, or Harz-Mountain; 'trio', and various choruses and voices. Here Faust is brought to a third degree of sensuality, the lowest state to which he descends. He then sees a vision foreboding Margareta's execution, but he is diverted by Mephistopheles with the Walpurgis Night's Dream, an 'Intermezzo'. (Satirical Masque, see Introduction.)

DESOLATE DAY: 187
Faust has learnt that Margareta is imprisoned, and he bitterly reproaches Mephistopheles.

NIGHT, OPEN COUNTRY: 189
(The shortest scene.) Faust and Mephistopheles galloping past gallows, to the rescue of Margareta.

PRISON: 189
Margareta is awaiting execution for the killing of her child. Faust pleads with her to go with him; but the strain has affected her mind. Mephistopheles summons them; Margareta commits her soul to Heaven, and Mephistopheles bears Faust away.

JOHANN WOLFGANG GOETHE

Born on 28th August 1749
at Frankfort-on-Main

BIOGRAPHICAL NOTE

In an old burgher-house, full of books and antiquities, Goethe had his first education from his father, a severe lawyer. His vivacious young mother supplied the fun. The boy came under French influence, through quartered officers and theatre, and later at Leipzig, where, at sixteen, he went to study Law. He led there a gay life, studied art, fell in love and, in 1768, returned ill, having written some lively lyrics and two small plays.

After convalescence, with deeply religious thought and some study of the occult, he went to Strasburg, where in two years he took his degree in Laws, was attracted to Medicine, and turned from lighter arts to the Germanic, to Shakespeare and to Folksong, influenced by Gothic splendour and by the young critic Herder. With his historic play, *Goetz*, and a tragic romance, *Werther*, Goethe was now hailed as leader of the Germans in their Romantic Revolt. Fiction in *Werther* was near enough to an actual love-triangle to start undying biographical curiosity. Goethe's lyric poetry was now of the greatest.

In 1775, Goethe was invited to Weimar, where Karl August soon made him Minister (Finance; Agriculture; Mines), and where love of Frau von Stein was to prove a main influence for the next twelve years.

In 1786 Goethe broke away to Italy, for nearly two years; and he realized so fully his longing for the calm strength of antiquity that his whole life was changed. Germany seemed to him still in 'Revolt' and immature. He now (1788) lived in semi-retirement with Christiane Vulpius (m. 1806), taking less part in public administration, except for the State Theatre, which he directed for over twenty years. He devoted himself to classical plays (e.g. *Iphigenie*, 1787; *Tasso*, 1790), to his *Faust* and to scientific work in Evolutionary Botany, Anatomy and Theory of Colour.

The death of Schiller (1805) ended nine inspiring years of friendship, the time of Goethe's great Ballads, of *Herman and Dorothea*, and of the finishing of his masterpiece, *Faust, Part One*.

The rest is quiet, strong work, the later *Wilhelm Meister*, *The Divan*, *Autobiography*, *Conversations* (Eckermann) and *Part Two* of *Faust*, finished in the poet's last years.

Goethe died on 22nd March 1832.

INTRODUCTION

I

GOETHE lived to the age of eighty-two, and we know that the figure of Faust persisted in his thoughts for a period of sixty years, practically the whole of his working life. The *First Part* of his *Faust* is his masterpiece. It was begun when Goethe was in his early twenties, and finished, except for a few lines, in 1801, when he was fifty-one. *Part Two*, with which we are not here concerned, did not receive its finishing touches until the poet's eighty-third year; it is a complex work of idealism, removed from the human conflict of conscience and love that the poet gives us in *Part One*, with an ardour and a vivacity of temperament for which he has been idolized, in his own country and elsewhere. It is the union of passion and wisdom in *Faust, Part One* that places Goethe among the master-poets of the world.

Idolatry is a disservice to any great writer, especially when the incense-burners, as in Goethe's case, have familiar access to his personal affairs. After all, their smoke is not his work. The few giants whom Goethe, across the centuries, has undoubtedly joined – Homer, Dante, Shakespeare – are free from such personal disquisitions; but Goethe's amazing activities as a poet, minister of state, theatre director, critic and man of science stand in a searching light of records and conversations hardly equalled in all literature. Even his intimate life is open; for, as Thomas Mann remarks, schoolboys learn his love-affairs by heart, like Jove's.

That man seems the more formidable who can step from so much table-talk into the small incomparable group of the immortals. Towards the end of his life Goethe did indeed assume something of an Olympian aloofness, to protect himself from busybodies; but in a modern perspective the great man can be seen as kindly-affectioned and even shy; and nothing could please him more than the world-wide acceptance of his *Faust* in men's hearts. In his youth as in his age, Goethe looked on life with strong ironic scrutiny; but he kept his warmth of heart as well, and in his modesty he offered his great work to his fellow-men as would a loving comrade. Faust, in his first scene with Wagner, insists on the value of sincerity, without which cleverness is nothing; and when, in the vision dedicatory to his poems, Goethe makes the Goddess rebuke him for any tendency to set himself apart as a super-man, he submits the question sincerely,

> *Why have I sought my path with fervent care,*
> *If not in hope to bring my brothers there?*

II

THE paths of Goethe's inner being, of his wit and of his passion, are vivid in his *Faust*; and it was one of the world's most fortunate inspirations that drew his genius to the old legend. He had already pondered on it when, at the age of twenty-four, a chronicle drama in prose, *Goetz von Berlichingen*, brought him at once into national fame (1773). For him it could have been a wrong turning. Though he was hailed as a leader for his stirring drama of freedom, he knew that it was not his true way to adopt historical themes, as it were, from the outside: Goethe always depended on original impulses from his own intimate experience, which his poetic conception was then to body forth again in universal terms. In common with the greatest of poets, his imagination is not shy of concrete things: images of real life leap forward at his call, so bearing his feelings that they 'readily come home to men's bosoms'. The outline for *Hamlet* Shakespeare might borrow, but the touching images,

> *Or ere those shoes were old*
> *With which she followed my poor father's body,*

came from his own burning love of simple things; and so it is with Goethe. 'Grasshopper', 'dust-bin', 'plank', and even 'pie-frills' serve the strong heart of his poetry. To quote again the penetrative novelist-critic Thomas Mann, 'Goethe himself is a wonderful instance of the fact that the purest naiveté and the most mighty understanding can go hand in hand' – a good recipe for a classic, but the product is rare. The astonishing thing is that, with all the tenderness and fire of youth, Goethe developed so early a superb clarity of judgment. His ripeness for his greatest theme was fourfold. He had already the finest command of lyrical expression that Germany has known; early encounter with the romance of sex had brought him face to face with the far-reaching ethical responsibilities of love; he had perceived the arrogance of human learning; and lastly, he had committed himself devotedly to a poet's life-long challenge of the mystery of existence. We know that Goethe weighed in his mind several stories as possible vehicles of his longings and beliefs; but the Faust legend took increasingly powerful form in his imagination, and the strength of his young genius is seen in the resolution with which he remoulded the story.

III

THE first Faust-Book was a good printer's thriller, published in 1587. It mingled fact and fiction. The old shadowy Faust, who lost his life in a demonstration of flying, seems to hark back in tradition to the sorcerer Simon, of *Acts*, Chapter viii; the name of Faust was assumed a second time, however, by a practising magician who worked sensational wonders and died, more scandalously, in 1537, and he is the hero of the German Faust-Book, published fifty years after his death. Goethe did not see this book of 1587, but Marlowe did, very quickly, and adopted it perhaps before it was translated. Here the story takes on special interest for English readers. The chief purveyors of drama in Germany, in the early seventeenth century, were the English Players, and they took over with them Marlowe's *Faust*. In the course of years the play became a receptacle for pantomime; but the marionette theatre took it up, and it was this puppet Faust that first kindled the imagination of Goethe, when a boy, in Frankfort.

Goethe, it seems, worked upon a later version of the popular Faust-Book, and much has been written concerning the motifs existing in the legend and those identical or additional in Goethe's mind. The chief threads are clear enough. In ages of scepticism, like our own, men disowning religion have been impatient with all barriers of convention, and have sought to satisfy their vague hunger by grasping at occult powers that seemed to lie beyond the ken of pedant authority. This was an impulse that Goethe, always assailed by a sense of unfulfilled longing, could feel in the sceptical 'Age of Enlightenment', as the known Faust had in the ferment of the Renaissance.

At twenty years of age, Goethe had to return home ill and dispirited from his studies at Leipzig, and it was now that he gave some attention to alchemy and black magic (the curious terms on p. 65 refer to certain substances and vessels of alchemy, of which he then read in Paracelsus). At the same time, however, the religious influence of a family friend, Fräulein von Klettenberg, convinced him of the inevitability of evil in life's pilgrimage; and he no doubt began then to invest the fate of Faust with spiritual values quite beyond the old crudities of devilry and punishment. His wisdom ripened swiftly; while his quick sense of irony remained, and was to remain, through his long life. Thus, a strong-minded undergraduate may well gird at the professors, as Goethe does in Faust's first soliloquy, and still more in the discourse of Dr Mephistopheles to the Freshman; but the marvel is that the very young Goethe unmasked pedantry with such lasting deep wisdom. Youth's challenging disrespect of the world speaks in the irony of Goethe's devil. In Faust himself the sceptical spirit is grave and mature, except when he is goaded to bitterness; in any case one must not identify Goethe with Faust any more than with Mephistopheles, for their creator was bigger than the two of them. The passionate Goethe had a humility and a control that he leaves for the most part undisclosed in his male heroes; and Goethe intended egotism as Faust's fault. Not only does he say to the mighty Earth Spirit

> *My name is Faust, in everything thy equal,*

but he forgets his snubbing and claims much later the Spirit's power again. An egotist, he impinges fatally on the admiring simplicity of Margareta, and therein is his guilt.

A restless groping for power is undoubtedly present in Faust and is largely his undoing; but in Goethe himself the boundless aspiration for a fulfilment above mortal reach was countered by an indomitable energy, that looked upon any static sentiment as weakness. The necessity of action has for him an almost religious value. When Faust settles earnestly in his study to review the 'Word' of St John (I. 1), it is 'The Deed' that is extolled. In his compact with Mephistopheles, Faust is only to be truly damned if the devil can lure him to unprogressive satisfactions,

> *If to the fleeting hour I say*
> *'Remain, so fair thou art, remain!'*

This seduction Mephistopheles, the Spirit of Negation, never actually achieves; and it is Goethe whose conviction cries out, in a poem called *Testament*,

> *Only the fruitful thing is true.*

IV

FAUST, PART ONE, though it has a strong and famous story, is very unconventional in its shape as a play. The struggle in Faust's mind, and his trenchant commentary on our life, provide absorbing speeches for the reader rather than for the stage, which requires a special adaptation of the drama. Goethe himself was sceptical about any theatrical success for his masterpiece, and it is easy to prove that he intended a big dramatic poem rather than a stage play: for instance, the poet does not so much as mention that a year has passed between Valentine's death and the Walpurgis Night, nor does he enumerate acts or scenes or *dramatis personae* (the present Contents Page is therefore amplified a little to help new readers more readily to a perspective). It is interesting to note that no public performance of the great *Part One* was given until the poet's eightieth year. A further performance in Weimar, for his eightieth birthday, had a striking success, due in no small measure to concentrated coaching by Goethe himself.

Later generations, brought up on Gounod's condensed version, must remember that Goethe's chief actor is the troubled human soul common to us all, seeking for courage upon our mysterious way, and for answer where none is easy to hear. Nevertheless the mystery culminates in the living tenderness of Gretchen; and it is in this theme that the young poet most of all vindicates his faith in the cogent truth of his own inward experience.

Here it seems well to give a brief lay-out of the artistic growth of the great work, for readers who are interested; but those who do not like such literary embryology may care to pass on to section five.

Goethe had been early attracted by a feature of the old legend in which Faust conjured up the lovely Helen of Troy, and this crude piece of virtuosity was transmuted in his mind to a realization of the pure spirit of Hellenic Art – though the old story frankly aimed at nothing more than a prize for voluptuous enjoyment. This Helen-motif persisted in Goethe's thoughts, and she appears later, in *Part Two*, with an involved aesthetical significance; but, in the youthful poet's *Part One*, his simple and deserted Gretchen has ousted from his mind Helen and all things fabulous, to make his masterpiece. The depth of feeling on which he drew relates to early love that he never forgot. There was an actual Gretchen in his boyhood, an unhappy encounter with a peasant girl, whose sweet nature was corrupted by bad surroundings; and male conscience had matured in him through his passionate love and desertion of Friederike Brion, daughter of a village pastor in Sesenheim, near Strasburg – 'Here I learnt what it was to be guilty'.

Goethe's first version of *Faust* was written from 1773 to 1775; and it contains the whole of the Gretchen story, together with Faust's first scene, the Freshman, and Auerbach's Cellar. Goethe took this original version with him to Weimar in 1775; but it was laid aside during eleven years of ministerial duties, and two further periods of work were needed before the full *Part One* was finished. Goethe turned to the work a second time when he was leaving Weimar in 1786, and the next four years saw additions, including some of Faust's demands on Mephistopheles (pp. 90–93), most of the 'Forest and Cavern', and all of the 'Witch's Kitchen'; this last was written in Italy, when Goethe had broken away from his years of administration in the impoverished State of Weimar; and a candid confession to his good Duke, Karl August, shows that he perceived more clearly in Rome the cold heartlessness underlying sensuality, so mordantly portrayed in his Mephistopheles.*

In a third period, 1797 to 1801, with the encouragement of Schiller, Goethe filled what he called the 'big gap' between Wagner's first exit and the Freshman's scene; that is to say, he wrote here the scenes of Easter Dawn and Easter-Day, the mysterious Poodle, and the Wager with Mephisto. Now were added, moreover, the Dedication, the Theatre Prelude, the Prologue and the Walpurgis Night, or Witches' Festival. Last touches, for publication in 1808, included the voice at the end – it seems like an echo – saving poor Margareta. It would be a pity if 'quick censure,

* This point is raised in Lowes Dickinson and Stawell, *Goethe and Faust*, a thoughtful analysis to which I am indebted in many ways.

acerbity, gifts of youth rather than of age' mistook the strength of this ending for weakness. Goethe was not pandering to optimism with a 'happy ending'. No man faced more thoroughly than he the depths of despair, even as he knew the heights of joy. Looking back, when he was past sixty, on that time of his *Werther* and the young *Faust*, he wrote very earnestly to his bereaved friend Zelter, 'I know full well what it cost me then, in effort and in resolution, to escape the waters of death, even as I have had since then to save myself from many another shipwreck by toiling effort and difficult recovery'. The letter throws a significant light on Faust's despair on the Easter dawning; but natural to this poet was a courage that did not believe ultimately in unresolved discords.

One of the severe artistic tasks of the third period was the transmutation of the perilous finale, the Prison Scene, from prose into verse. The drinking scene in Auerbach's Cellar had been similarly brought over, and a comparison of the boisterous roughness of the drinkers with the poignant simplicity of the finale reveals the poet's sureness of hand.

V

THE verse of Goethe bends beautifully to his thought. He was Germany's foremost lyric poet, as well as her greatest man; but the daring course of the verse in *Faust* ventures far from the lyric. Sometimes the lines are classical in austere and lofty music, sometimes they run in a short swaying of romantic impulse. Any translation in sober prose, for instance, of what the Spirits say (p. 78) will remain outside Goethe's country, with no passport – for here is incantation. On the other hand there are hundreds of lines to which Goethe gives the sinew of his thought without any desire for colour or voluptuous attraction. Margareta speaks with an intense, one can say unique, simplicity, that menaces a translator with constant peril of bathos; and Mephistopheles is boldly collo-

Introduction

quial, as he himself says in his audacious apology to the Lord God. Apologies of translators, to anybody, are usually tedious; but the English reader will tune-in to Goethe the better if he remembers, please, two points. First the German language is on the whole homelier than English. Secondly, Goethe shows masterly genius in an old form neglected here until recent years, a form of easy-going rough verse, usually in couplets with four stresses, much as in our *Hudibras*. If a surprised reader asks, Did so great a man then write in doggerel? the answer is in the affirmative; he not only wrote but revelled in it. The form is well known in Germany by the name of *Knüttelvers*. Goethe has turns reminiscent of early plain poets, particularly Hans Sachs; but it is interesting to find that his mother, whom he adored,* was familiar with the tradition, and actually put *Knüttelvers* in her letters; the genius of her son made of it a new and most flexible weapon of wit.

There is, as Goethe pre-eminently knew, a great poetry that requires the fusion of ecstasy with form, whereby rhythm has its sanction and is wedded to meaning; but there is another poetry where verve of wit takes the place of feeling and calls out for rhythm, has a right to it, to make its vivacity effective. Thus the idiom is intentionally unbeautiful in such an opening as

> *My worthy Sir, you view affairs*
> *Like other people, I'm afraid;*
> *But we, more cunning in our cares,*
> *Must take our joys before they fade.* (p. 91)

For poetry, which Milton said should be simple, sensuous and passionate, the whole passage is as thin as bay-rum. Fortunately for our human interest, Goethe did not pretend to stay all the time on

---

* From Father came life's earnest poise,
   A bearing strict and stable;
   From Mother dear, my sense of joys
   And will to spin a fable.

peaks of emotion; and such lines are healthily astringent, I hope, coming as they do from the devil.

VI

It is perhaps an easy saying, but it has its depth, that cynicism is the only sin. This devil of Goethe's must be known to be appreciated. He is the world's most convincing portrait of Satan, and cynicism, scoffing, negation, is the key-note of his intellectuality. Mephistopheles thrives on the young poet's formidable diagnosis of the inherent folly of our life. Scholars, such as Erich Schmidt and Georg Witkowski, have pointed out that even his use of slang and of foreign words is part of his fundamental mode of disrespect. He is more modern than yesterday. To-day's typist encounters him if she finds, to her secret resentment, that in the office any word of aspiration is at once twisted with a grin into smut. It seems that Satan has present activity with an ancient title; for the old word *diabolos* turns out to have, before our history, the same root as ballistics, and means, roughly, 'mud-slinger'. If the office now laughs, it may well pause to realize that Mephistopheles himself remarks upon mankind's being by no means better off for abolishing him as a spook. Twice Mephistopheles gives direct parody of sex, once of its high romantic aspiration, and once of the alluring stir of what is now knowingly called *libido*; in which passage, by the way, I am grateful for the dignity of Penguins, for other editions print dashes, leaving innocent souls to guess far worse things than Goethe wrote. The mockery of Mephistopheles, however, easily returns to the attack:

> *Ah, now you're put about*
> *And claim the moral right to cry 'For shame',*
> *Because chaste ears must never hear the name*
> *Of things chaste hearts can never go without.*

Goethe has given the world the very devil.

VII

THAT a great man should have a great sense of humour is not surprising; but it was not always realized that the enthroned Sage of Weimar could be simply an 'enfant terrible' of authorship. He could laugh at himself. He called his greatest work hybrid. He looked at his own creation of a monster, swelling from behind the stove (p. 72), and wrote to Schiller, 'The devil I am conjuring up takes on alarmingly'. But he could do much worse than this, as can be proved if one is allowed a demure note upon Herr Nicolai's buttocks – apart from the oddity, a critical valuation is involved; and the reader is at least saved from Notes at the back of the book.

Of the curious verses concerning Sir Runic Rump (p. 177) one needs to know that a self-important critic, Nicolai, duly hating the supernatural, as was proper in a minor prophet of the 'Aufklärung' (Enlightenment or 'Explaining Away'), had attacked Goethe sharply, only to be overtaken by an illness in which he himself saw phantoms. Nicolai then announced his cure, and solemnly published the method, namely the application of leeches to his backside. This was a little too much for Goethe; but how, says the serious reader, how can he bring such items into his mightiest work?

The truth is that the spirit of phantasy on the Brocken, or Harz-Mountain, where he sets his Witches' Walpurgis orgy, originally prompted Goethe to an even larger plan in devilish discourse, including the holding of a satanic court; while the fire-fly verses, strung together in the queer Intermezzo, were first designed for quite another publication, satirizing fops and vanities in literature and society.* Since the Brocken scenes required devilments to distract Faust from the tragic human truth, as he afterwards indignantly says, Goethe thought they might as well have these.

* Nobody will now want a detailed key; but Nicolai reappears in his role of traveller and Jesuit hater; the Mieding named was a stage-manager in Weimar; Hennings a critic; and Tegel a haunted manor near Berlin.

Over this Oberon-Titania Intermezzo there have been head-shakings, even among the professors; some have been bold enough to deplore it, or even to leave it out. It is said that the subsequent indignation of Faust, referred to above, is hardly a strong enough link or bridge back to the tragedy; but Goethe may have intended a chasm; else why did he leave that one following scene in prose? We can accept the devilment, topical or not, and be thankful for the strength of the great story, bearing as it does the question that touches us all, as to what our self-will is doing, upon our path through eternity.

But why, it may be asked, is the great and echoing duel between human aspiration and despair focussed on a simple love-affair with a humble girl? Are not these two very different things?

The unity is in Goethe's strong personality, where sex was a tribunal of self. If selfishness is a destroyer, then is its action most fatal when it touches that whose very life is of the opposite nature, love. Goethe holds that the true action of love lies in a willing death of self, whereby life is saved, in a richer continuity. Goethe had every reason to know very much about love, both in its depth and in its enchanting approaches – compassing in its possibilities, as he wrote to Charlotte von Stein, the steadfastness of a star or the flicker of wild-fire – and he had deep convictions about the significance of first surrender. His age was as sceptical as ours. Clever Ones who, upon some acquaintance with physiology and psychology, regard virginity as a mere inconvenience, may receive his compliment (p. 185) but not his agreement with a position philosophically poor, seeing that Nature proposes no obliging abolition of virginity, and that wisdom thinks our life to be inwrought with many symbols that we do not fully comprehend. The ecstasy of fulfilment that has power to call forth another living soul remains our chief mystery; and, despite the cleverness of men and of Mephistopheles, nothing has more significance for human fate than the question as to whether a true fulfilment can abide the presence of egotism. This was the question in Goethe's mind when he so fundamentally re-cast the old legend of Faust.

The Helen of *Part Two* is no human being: her union with Faust is the marriage of Classical with Romantic Art – with other devices of allegory. In *Part One* we have an altogether different thing. The whole Gretchen story, it must be remembered, was taken over from Goethe's early work practically unaltered. In that spring of life the poet's mind was reaching out for form, even as his strong young soul was assimilating its human trouble, its fate and its longing; then came the prime of life, years that added mature and passionate reflection; so that this story of the little pawnbroker's daughter, even in the teeth of devilish comment, now holds the admiration of the world.

At the end of the prolix *Part Two* Faust is saved by his will to strive, and is claimed by the spirit of Gretchen. Those who look for that logical ending, and for the religious wisdom of the old poet's mind, will support Goethe's very natural wish that the work of his age should not be separated from that of his youthful prime. But posterity has judged otherwise; and G. H. Lewes, who, by his *Life*, has done more for Goethe than any other Englishman, had the courage to state the reasons nearly a hundred years ago. He warns us that *Part Two* has not enough human interest to hold us, whereas *Part One*, for a first reading, has perhaps too much. 'It has every element: wit, pathos, wisdom, farce, mystery, melody, reverence, doubt, magic and irony.' Lewes made his list with conscious enthusiasm; but the truth of it is enough to account for the never-ending appeal of Goethe's *Faust* to the minds of all sorts of readers, both learned and unlearned.

London, 1949. P.W.

FAUST

PART ONE

DEDICATION

Once more you hover near me, forms and faces
    Seen long ago with troubled youthful gaze.
And shall I this time hold you, limn the traces,
    Fugitive still, of those enchanted days?
You closer press: then take your powers and places,
    Command me, rising from the murk and haze;
Deep stirs my heart, awakened, touched to song,
As from a spell that flashes from your throng.

You bear the glass of days that were glad-hearted;
    Dear memories, beloved shades arise;
Like an old legendary echo started,
    Come friendship and first love before my eyes.
Old sorrow stirs, the wounds again have smarted,
    Life's labyrinth before my vision lies,
Disclosing dear ones who, by fortune cheated,
Passed on their way, of love and light defeated.

They cannot hear what now I bring, belated,
    Who listened to the early tunes I made:
Gone is the throng by love so animated,
    Dead the responsive tribute that they paid.
My tragic theme rings out, for strangers fated,
    For strange applause that makes me half afraid.
The rest, who held my music sweet and cherished,
Stray through the world dispersed, or they have perished.

Now comes upon me long forgotten yearning
    For the sweet solemn tryst those spirits keep.
I feel the trembling words of song returning,

    Like airs that softly on the harp-strings creep.
The stern heart softens, all its pride unlearning,
    A shudder passes through me, and I weep.
All that I have stands off from me afar,
And all I lost is real, my guiding-star.

PRELUDE IN THE THEATRE

Director. Poet. Comedian.

DIRECTOR. You two, Sirs, who have been my stay
　In many a time of storm and stress,
　What does our theatre want to-day,
　What are our chances of success?
　To please the good old public I've elected,
　Who live and let live – them I'd recreate.
　The boards are firm, the scaffold is erected,
　And, open-eyed, the people sit and wait;
　A rare dramatic treat is now expected:
　They take for granted that it's something great.
　I know my public, how it is impressed,
　Yet feel, I must confess, my hopes receding;
　For, even if they seldom see the best,
　The worthy folk go in so much for reading.
　How can we manage something brisk and new,
　Not only smart, but edifying too?
　For, frankly, nothing pleases me much more
　Than sight of crowds, when they begin to pour
　Wave upon wave, at half-past three or four,
　In daylight through our strait and narrow door;
　Or when they shove and fight towards the wicket,
　And nearly break their necks to get a ticket,
　With frantic elbowing and furious looks,
　Like starving beggars round a pastry-cook's.
　To work such wide enchantment – who can doubt it? –
　You, poet, are the man, so set about it.
POET. Speak not to me about the motley rabble,
　Whose sight no inspiration can abide.

Preserve me from the tumult and the babble,
That sweeps us helpless in its vulgar tide.
Nay, bring me rather to that brink of heaven
Where flowers the poet's joy, serene and still,
Where love and friendship mingle, as the leaven
That god-like comes to quicken and fulfil.
Ay me, the deepest stirrings of emotion,
The thoughts that tremble on the murmuring lips,
Frail merchandise upon the poet's ocean,
The violence of a moment will eclipse.
For art may need long years of true devotion
To bring perfection to the light of day.
The brilliant passes, like the dew at morn;
The true endures, for ages yet unborn.

COMEDIAN. For my part, you can keep the unborn age;
Or, if we really have to talk about it,
Why, who would then delight our present stage,
That asks its fun, and will not go without it?
A fine young fellow to be entertained
Here, in the flesh, is not to be disdained.
The man with easy power to put it over
Blames not the public taste, but lives in clover.
He by whose art men's fiery thoughts are fanned
Rejoices in a sea of upturned faces.
Then courage, friends, show 'em the master-hand,
Let fancy fly, with all her lofty graces,
Pack wisdom in, with tenderness and passion,
But never put good fooling out of fashion.

DIRECTOR. Above all, give your play abundant action:
They want a show, then give them satisfaction.
Let plenty happen, right before their eyes,
So that the audience can stare in wonder,
So you are certain of the popular prize,

Prelude in the Theatre

    Your fortune's made, while still the plaudits thunder.
    It's crowded stuff you need, to grip the crowd;
    Then each good soul finds something to his liking.
    Give much, please many: the applause is loud,
    And each goes home and says the show is striking.
    Dished up with ease, made light as a caprice,
    A rich ragout, the mixture is what matters;
    Serve them a dozen pieces in the piece.
    Your perfect whole will have a short-lived lease:
    The public taste will tear it into tatters.
POET. But can't you feel how bad such products are?
    How, on an artist, such advice must jar?
    The bungling of each clever little fool
    You make your one artistic rule.
DIRECTOR. Censure like that disturbs me not a bit.
    And, as for what you say of fools,
    Remember, you have coarse-grained wood to split,
    So take the proper tools.
    And try to think for whom you write!
    Some come because they're bored by night,
    Or see no more in us than masks and capers.
    Some, curiosities excite;
    Some come from gluttony's delight,
    Or, what is worse, from following the papers.
    The ladies bring us fashion's gallery,
    And play their parts without a salary.
    And will you dream on your poetic peak,
    Or triumph if the play should prove a draw?
    Observe the patrons close, if truth you seek:
    One kind is cool, the other kind is raw.
    After the play, one man is all for cards,
    One for a wild night on a wench's breast:
    Roll you for this your heavenward regards,

Or dun the Muses with your high behest?
I tell you, pack your plays, and when you've packed 'em
You'll find, that way, you never go astray.
So write for people only to distract 'em:
To satisfy them's hopeless, anyway.
Why, what's upsetting you? Delight or anguish?
POET. Get hence, and find yourself another slave.
Or shall a poet be content to languish
In degradation of what heaven gave
To be his right? the highest human power
Frittered away to serve your little hour?
Whence comes his writ to summon every heart,
To bid the very elements obey him?
Whence, but from chimes that in his soul will start,
To harmonize the world that would betray him?
When Nature's thread, that filament never-ending,
Is nonchalantly on the distaff wound,
When unrelated things that know no blending
Send forth their vexed, uneasy jarring sound –
Who then bestows the rhythmic line euphonious,
The ordered pulse, to stir or soothe the soul?
Who marshals fragments to a ceremonious
And splendid music, universal, whole?
Who rides the flood of passion at its height?
Or sings the glow of evening, solemn, sweet?
Who strews the spring's dear garlands of delight
In petalled path for his beloved's feet?
Or who can twine the wreath for honour's portals,
Can insignificant leaves with tongues invest,
Assure Olympus, and unite immortals? –
The might of man, in poets manifest.
COMEDIAN. Well, use the wondrous inspirations, pray,
And set about the business straight away.

Prelude in the Theatre

Approach it as you would a love-affair:
You meet, you feel the spell, and linger there,
And by and by you think yourself enchanted.
At first you thrive; then obstacles are planted;
You walk on air, then fall to bittersweet:
And thus, behold, your romance is complete.
Now that's the stuff to make our play a charmer:
Plunge into life, and give them human drama.
The act is common, the perception's not;
So seize it, and you have a thrilling plot.
Give chequered scenes, though meaning may grow dimmer,
A chain of errors, and of truth a glimmer:
This is refreshing, here you have the brew
That quickens all the world, and sees us through.
Then gathers round the wisest flower of youth,
Then come the tender-hearted ones to sup;
Those see the play, and grasp its sacred truth,
These drink your drama's melancholy up.
One's roused by this, another finds that fit:
Each loves the play for what he brings to it.
The young are quick to mirth or tearful rapture,
Entranced by style and superficial pranks.
The mind that's formed, you'll have the deuce to capture:
The heart that's yet in growth will yield you thanks.

POET. Then bring me back the days of dreaming,
When I myself was yet unformed,
When song welled up in me, and teeming
The tuneful fancies in me swarmed.
I'd all the misty world before me,
And every bud with promise sprang,
And every valley, to restore me,

Burgeoned with blossom as I sang.
I nothing had, yet was not poor:
The spur of truth was mine, and fancy's lure.
Give me those days with heart in riot,
The depths of bliss that touched on pain,
The force of hate, and love's disquiet –
Ah, give me back my youth again!

COMEDIAN.
Your youth you need, my friend, when called to face
The onslaught of a foeman in the fight,
Or for an ardent lovely girl's embrace,
Who hangs upon your neck for love's delight;
Or youth would serve to win the sprinter's fame,
The goal, the laurels, glimmering from afar;
Or you might dance, perhaps, till daylight came,
Still young enough to toast the morning star.
But, ah, to strike the well-known chords with skill,
To set, with cunning aim, each heart a-throb,
And find the chosen mark at your sweet will,
That, Sirs, I take to be a veteran's job.
The more's the praise – you needn't take it ill:
It's not that age brings childhood back again,
Age merely shows what children we remain.

DIRECTOR. Enough of words, for, to be candid,
I'd like to see some work begun.
While all this pretty talk is bandied
We might have something useful done.
Why talk of mood, divine afflatus,
That ne'er to waverers occurs?
If you assume a poet's status,
Command me poetry, good Sirs!
You know our needs: we want a brew,
A liquor with some body in it.

Prelude in the Theatre

The process waits. Then up, begin it!
What's left to-day, to-morrow's still to do.
Lose not a day, but straight prepare,
And grasp your chance with resolute trust,
And take occasion by the hair,
For, once involved in the affair,
You'll carry on because you must.
The German stage lets each try what he may:
Then spare me nothing, on our special day,
Either of back-cloth or machinery.
Have sun and moon, and what you will of scenery.
And of the lesser fires be lavish:
Give 'em a star-light fit to ravish.
Of water, cliffs, romantic stuff,
And beasts and birds we cannot have enough.
Thus, on our narrow boards, shall you bestride
The whole Creation's prospect, far and wide,
And travel cunning, swift as thought can tell,
From Heaven through the world and down to hell.

PROLOGUE IN HEAVEN

*The Lord. The Hosts of Heaven. Afterwards Mephistopheles.
The three Archangels come forward.*

RAPHAEL. The day-star, sonorous as of old,
  Goes his predestined way along,
And round his path is thunder rolled,
  While sister-spheres join rival song.
New strength have angels at the sight,
  Though none may scan the infinitude,
And splendid, as in primal light,
  The high works of the world are viewed.
GABRIEL. Swift, unimaginably swift
  The glory of the earth rolls round,
And scenes of heavenly radiance shift
  To fearfulness of night profound;
By floods of sea in foaming forces
  Cliffs at their shuddering base are churned,
And flung in planetary courses
  The seas and cliffs are ever turned.
MICHAEL. And storms contend in angry fuming
  From sea to land, from land to sea,
A chain of raging force assuming,
  In their tempestuous majesty.
The flame of brilliant devastation
  Now lights the thunderbolt his way;
But angels, Lord, in adoration,
  Hail the sweet progress of thy day.
THE THREE. New strength have angels at the sight,
  Amazed at thy infinitude,
And splendid as in primal light
  Are all thy mighty works renewed.

MEPHISTOPHELES.
>   Since you, O Lord, are with us here once more,
>   To ask how we are going on at large,
>   And since you viewed me kindly heretofore,
>   I thought I'd make one, too, in the menage.
>   Your pardon, if my idiom is lowly,
>   My eloquence up here would meet with scorn,
>   Pathos from me would cause you laughter solely,
>   If laughter weren't a thing you have forsworn.
>   Your suns and worlds are not within my ken,
>   I merely watch the plaguey state of men.
>   The little god of earth remains the same queer sprite
>   As on the first day, or in primal light.
>   His life would be less difficult, poor thing,
>   Without your gift of heavenly glimmering;
>   He calls it Reason, using light celestial
>   Just to outdo the beasts in being bestial.
>   To me he seems, with deference to Your Grace,
>   One of those crickets, jumping round the place,
>   Who takes his flying leaps, with legs so long,
>   Then falls to grass and chants the same old song;
>   But, not content with grasses to repose in,
>   This one will hunt for muck to stick his nose in.

THE LORD. Have you no more to say to me?
>   Is plaint your one necessity?
>   Will nothing please you upon earth?

MEPHISTOPHELES.
>   No, Lord, I tell you frankly what it's worth:
>   It's bad; men drown in evils that are sent them;
>   Poor things, I find it boring to torment them.

THE LORD. Know you one Faust?
MEPHISTOPHELES.   The Doctor?
THE LORD.   Him, my servant.

Prologue in Heaven

MEPHISTOPHELES.
> Indeed, Lord, a retainer strange and fervent:
> From any earthly victuals he'll refrain,
> His fever drives him to a lofty plane.
> In madness, half suspected on his part,
> He hankers after heaven's loveliest orbs,
> Demands from earth the choicest joy and art,
> And, far and near, what pleases and absorbs
> Still fails to satisfy his restless heart.

THE LORD.
> Though now he serves me in bewildered ways,
> My light shall lead him soon from his despairing.
> Does not the grower see in leafy days
> His sapling's years of blossom and of bearing?

MEPHISTOPHELES.
> What will you wager that you do not lose him,
> Supposing always you will not demur
> About my guiding him in paths I choose him?

THE LORD. You shall have leave to do as you prefer,
> So long as earth remains his mortal dwelling;
> For man must strive, and striving he must err.

MEPHISTOPHELES.
> My thanks, O Lord. For frankly it's repelling
> To have so much to do with the deceased.
> For me a glowing cheek is like a feast.
> I'm not at home to corpses in my house:
> There's something in me of the cat-and-mouse.

THE LORD. Let it be so: to you is given the power
> That may seduce this soul from his true source,
> And drag him down with you, in fatal hour,
> If you can wholly bend him to your force.
> But stand ashamed when called on to confess:
> A good man in his dark, bewildered course

Will not forget the way of righteousness.
MEPHISTOPHELES. Agreed. My purpose is a likely horse,
And little doubt I make of my success.
But if I win, then clearly give me best,
A proper triumph, fanfares by the dozen.
Dust shall he bite, ay, lick it up with zest,
Just like the snake, my celebrated cousin.
THE LORD. In that you also have a dispensation.
Your kindred never had my hate or scorn:
Of all the spirits of negation
The rogue is least of burdens to be borne.
Man's efforts sink below his proper level,
And since he seeks for unconditioned ease,
I send this fellow, who must goad and tease
And toil to serve creation, though a devil.
But ye, true sons of heaven, shall delight
In the full wealth of living beauty's sight.
Eternal Growth, fulfilment, vital, sure,
Enwrap your minds in love's immortal folds,
And all that life in floating semblance holds,
Stablish it fast, in thought that shall endure.
  (*The heaven closes, the Archangels depart.*)
MEPHISTOPHELES (*alone*).
I like to see the Governor now and then,
And take good care to keep relations civil.
It's decent in the first of gentlemen
To speak so friendly, even to the devil.

THE TRAGEDY

NIGHT · FAUST'S STUDY (i)

*In a high-vaulted, narrow, gothic chamber,
Faust is discovered restless at his desk.*

FAUST. Philosophy have I digested,
The whole of Law and Medicine,
From each its secrets I have wrested,
Theology, alas, thrown in.
Poor fool, with all this sweated lore,
I stand no wiser than I was before.
Master and Doctor are my titles;
For ten years now, without repose,
I've held my erudite recitals
And led my pupils by the nose.
And round we go, on crooked ways or straight,
And well I know that ignorance is our fate,
And this I hate.
I have, I grant, outdistanced all the others,
Doctors, pedants, clergy and lay-brothers;
All plague of doubts and scruples I can quell,
And have no fear of devil or of hell,
And in return am destitute of pleasure,
Knowing that knowledge tricks us beyond measure,
That man's conversion is beyond my reach,
Knowing the emptiness of what I teach.
Meanwhile I live in penury,
No worldly honour falls to me.
No dog would linger on like this,
And so I turn to the abyss
Of necromancy, try if art

Can voice or power of spirits start,
To do me service and reveal
The things of Nature's secret seal,
And save me from the weary dance
Of holding forth in ignorance.
Then shall I see, with vision clear,
How secret elements cohere,
And what the universe engirds,
And give up huckstering with words.

   O silver majesty of night,
Moon, look no more upon my plight,
You whom my eyes at midnight oft
Have gazed upon, when slow and soft
You crossed my papers and my books
With friendly, melancholy looks.
Would that my soul could tranquil stray
On many a moonlit mountain way,
By cavernous haunts with ghostly shadows,
Or thread the silver of the meadows,
Released from learning's smoky stew
To lave me in the moonlit dew.

   But, ah, this prison has my soul,
Damnable, bricked-in, cabined hole,
Where even the heaven's dear light must pass
Saddened through the painted glass.
Hemmed in with stacks of books am I,
Where works the worm with dusty mange,
While to the vaulted roof on high
The smoky ranks of papers range;
Retorts and jars my crib encumber,
And crowded instruments and, worse,
Loads of hereditary lumber –
And this, ay this, is called my universe.

Night

And shall I wonder why my heart
Is lamed and frightened in my breast,
Why all the springs of life that start
Are strangely smothered and oppressed?
Instead of all that life can hold
Of Nature's free, god-given breath,
I take to me the smoke and mould
Of skeletons and dust and death.
Up and away! A distant land
Awaits me in this secret book
From Nostradamus' very hand,
Nor for a better guide I look.
Now shall I read the starry pole,
In Nature's wisdom shall I seek
And know, with rising power of soul,
How spirit doth to spirit speak.
No dusty logic can divine
The meaning of a sacred sign.
Mysterious spirits, hovering near,
Answer me, if now ye hear!

(*He opens the book and lights upon the Sign of the Macrocosm.*)

Ah, strangely comes an onset of delight,
Invading all my senses as I gaze:
Young, sacred bliss-of-life springs at the sight,
And fires my blood in all its branching ways.
Was it a god who made this mystic scroll,
To touch my spirit's tumult with its healing,
And fill my wretched heart with joyous feeling,
And bring the secret world before my soul,
The hidden drive of Nature's force revealing?
Myself a god? — With lightened vision's leap
I read the riddle of the symbols, hear

The looms of Nature's might, that never sleep,
And know at last things spoken of the seer:
"'Tis not the spirit world is sealed;
Thy heart is dead, thy senses' curtain drawn.
But, scholar, bathe, rejoicing, healed,
Thy earthly breast in streams of roseate dawn.'
          (*He studies the sign.*)
Lo, single things inwoven, made to blend,
To work in oneness with the whole, and live
Members one of another, while ascend
Celestial powers, who ever take and give
Vessels of gold on heaven's living stair,
Their pinions fragrant with the bliss they bear,
Pervading all, that heaven and earth agree,
Transfixing all the world with harmony.
    O endless pageant! – But a pageant still,
A show, that mocks my touch or grasp or will!
Where are the nipples, Nature's springs, ah where
The living source that feeds the universe?
You flow, you give to drink, mysterious nurse,
And yet my soul is withered in despair.
    (*Disconsolately he turns the pages until his glance rests on the sign of the Spirit of Earth.*)
A curious change affects me in this sign:
You, kindred Sprite of Earth, come strangely nearer;
My spirits rise, my powers are stronger, clearer,
As from the glow of a refreshing wine.
I gather heart to risk the world's encounter,
To bear my human fate as fate's surmounter,
To front the storm, in joy or grief not palter,
Even in the gnash of shipwreck never falter.
    The clouds close in above me
And hidden is the moon;

Night 47

The lamp dies down.
A vapour grows – red quiverings
Dart round my head – there creeps
A shuddering from the vaulted roof
And seizes me!
I know, dread spirit of my call, 'tis you.
Stand forth, disclosed!
Ah, how my heart is harrowed through!
In tumult of feeling
My mind is riven, my senses reeling.
To you I yield, nor care if I am lost.
This thing must be, though life should be the cost.
    (*He seizes the book and pronounces the secret sign of the Spirit. A reddish flame shoots up, and the Spirit appears in the flame.*)

SPIRIT. Who calls on me?
FAUST (*turning away*).   O fearful form!
SPIRIT.   At length
  You have compelled me here. Your strength
  Has wrestled long about my sphere,
  And now –
FAUST.   I tremble: come not near.
SPIRIT. With bated breath you laboured to behold me,
  To hear my voice, to see me face to face.
  You prayed with might, with depth that has controlled me,
  And here am I! – What horror now can chase
  The colour from your lips, my superman?
  Where the soul's cry? The courage that began
  To shape a world, and bear and foster it?
  The heart that glowed, with lofty ardour lit,
  To claim ethereal spirits as your peers?
  Are you that Faust whose challenge smote my ears,

Who beat his way to me, proclaimed his hour,
And trembles now in presence of my power,
Writhes from the breath of it, a frightened worm?
FAUST. And shall I, thing of flame, flinch at the sequel?
My name is Faust, in everything your equal.
SPIRIT. In flood of life, in action's storm
I ply on my wave
With weaving motion
Birth and the grave,
A boundless ocean,
Ceaselessly giving
Weft of living,
Forms unending,
Glowing and blending.
So work I on the whirring loom of time,
The life that clothes the deity sublime.
FAUST. Swift Spirit, you whose projects have no end,
How near akin our natures seem to be!
SPIRIT. You match the spirit that you comprehend,
Not me. (*He vanishes.*)
FAUST (*filled with dismay*). Not you!
Whom then?
I, made in God's own image,
And not with you compare! (*A knock.*)
Damnation, that will be my Servitor!
My richest hope is in confusion hurled:
He spoils my vision of the spirit world,
This lickspittle of learning at my door.
(*Wagner in dressing-gown and night-cap, carrying a lamp.
Faust turns reluctantly.*)
WAGNER. Beg pardon, but I heard you, Sir, declaiming –
Some tragedy, I'll warrant, from the Greek? –
That's just the learned art at which I'm aiming,

For people are impressed when scholars speak.
Indeed, I've heard the stage can be a teacher,
So that the actor can inspire the preacher.
FAUST. Past question, if the parson is a mummer –
A thing you may discover, now and then.
WAGNER. But, Sir, if learning ties us, winter, summer,
With holiday so rare, that we see men
As through a glass, remote and ill-defined,
How shall our counsel serve to lead mankind?
FAUST. If feeling fails you, vain will be your course,
And idle what you plan unless your art
Springs from the soul with elemental force
To hold its sway in every listening heart.
Well, well, keep at it: ply the shears and paste,
Concoct from feasts of other men your hashes,
And should the thing be wanting fire or taste,
Blow into flame your little heap of ashes:
You'll find some apes and children who'll admire,
If admiration is your chief desire;
But what is uttered from the heart alone
Will win the hearts of others to your own.
WAGNER. Yet by his style a speaker stands to win;
That I know well, and that I'm backward in.
FAUST. Trust honesty, to win success,
Be not a noisy jingling fool.
Good sense, Sir, and rightmindedness
Have little need to speak by rule.
And if your mind on urgent truth is set,
Need you go hunting for an epithet?
Nay, these your polished speeches that you make,
Serving mankind your snipped-out pie-frill papers,
They nourish us no more than winds that shake
The withered leaves, or shred the autumnal vapours.

WAGNER. Ah me, Sir, long indeed is art;
  Our life is very short, however,
  And often, in my studious endeavour
  A fearful dread assails my head and heart.
  How hard it is to master ways and means
  By which a man may reach the fountain-head!
  And, ere he's half-way there, fate intervenes:
  Before he knows it, the poor devil's dead.
FAUST. Is parchment, then, your well of living water,
  Where whosoever drinks shall be made whole?
  Look not to stem your craving in that quarter:
  The spring is vain that flows not from the soul.
WAGNER. The pleasure, by your leave, is great, to cast
  The mind into the spirit of the past,
  And scan the former notions of the wise,
  And see what marvellous heights we've reached at last.
FAUST. Most nobly have we, up to the starry skies!
  My friend, for us the alluring times of old
  Are like a book that's sealed-up sevenfold.
  And what you call the Spirit of the Ages
  Is but the spirit of your learned sages,
  Whose mirror is a pitiful affair,
  Shunned by mankind after a single stare,
  A mouldy dustbin, or a lumber attic,
  Or at the most a blood-and-thunder play
  Stuffed full of wit sententious and pragmatic,
  Fit for the sawdust puppetry to say.
WAGNER. And yet the world, the human heart and mind –
  To understand these things must be our aim.
FAUST. To understand – and how is that defined?
  Who dares to give that child its proper name?
  The few of understanding, vision rare,
  Who veiled not from the herd their hearts, but tried,

Night

Poor generous fools, to lay their feelings bare,
Them have men always burnt and crucified.
Excuse me, friend, it grows deep into night,
And now is time to think about adjourning.

WAGNER. I could have stayed up longer with delight,
To join in discourse with your lofty learning.
But, Sir, to-morrow comes our Easter Day,
When I shall ask more questions, if I may.
I've learnt a deal, made books my drink and meat,
But cannot rest till knowledge is complete. (*Exit.*)

FAUST.
How strange, that he who cleaves to shallow things
Can keep his hopes alive on empty terms,
And dig with greed for precious plunderings,
And find his happiness unearthing worms!

How dared this voice to raise its human bleat
Where waits the spirit world in immanent power?
And yet the man, so barren and effete,
Deserves my thanks in this most perilous hour.
He snatched me from a desperate despite
Fit to unhinge my reason, or to slay.
The apparition towered to such a height
My soul was dwarfed within me, in dismay.

I, God's own image, who have seemed, forsooth,
Near to the mirror of eternal truth,
Compassed the power to shed the mortal clay
And revel in the self's celestial day,
I, who presumed in puissance to out-soar
The cherubim, to flow in Nature's veins,
With god-like joy in my creative pains,
I rode too high, and deep must I deplore:
One thunder-word has robbed me of my reins.

I dare not, Spirit, count me in your sphere:

For, though I had the power to call you here,
No force have I that binds you or retains.
And in that moment dread and wondrous,
When I, so puny, grew so great,
You thrust me with a verdict thund'rous
Back to uncertain mortal fate.
Who is my guide? What shall I shun?
Or what imperious urge obey?
Alas, not only woes, but actions done,
Walk by us still, to hedge us on our way.

    The spirit's splendour, in the soul unfurled,
Is ever stifled with a stranger stuff.
High values, matched with good things of this world,
Mocking recede, and seem an airy bluff.
Our nobler veins, the true, life-giving springs,
Are choked with all the dust of earthy things.

    What though imagination spread her wings
In early hope towards the things eternal,
Shrunk is her spacious realm in the diurnal
Defeat that loss and disappointment brings.
Full soon in deepest hearts care finds a nest,
And builds her bed of pain, in secret still,
There rocks herself, disturbing joy and rest,
And ever takes new shapes to work her will,
With fluttering fears for home or wife or child,
A thought of poison, flood or perils wild;
For man must quail at bridges never crossed,
Lamenting even things he never lost.

    Shall I then rank with gods? Too well I feel
My kinship with the worm, who bores the soil,
Who feeds on dust until the wanderer's heel
Gives sepulture to all his care and toil.

    Is it not dust, that fills my hundred shelves,

Night

And walls me in like any pedant hack?
Fellow of moth that flits and worm that delves,
I drag my life through learned bric-a-brac.
And shall I here discover what I lack,
And learn, by reading countless volumes through,
That mortals mostly live on misery's rack,
That happiness is known to just a few?
You hollow skull, what has your grin to say,
But that a mortal brain, with trouble tossed,
Sought once, like mine, the sweetness of the day,
And strove for truth, and in the gloam was lost.
You instruments, you mock me to my face,
With wheel and gimbal, cylinder and cog;
You were my key to unlock the secret place:
The wards are cunning, but the levers clog.
For Nature keeps her veil inviolate,
Mysterious still in open light of day,
And where the spirit cannot penetrate
Your screws and irons will never make a way.
Here stands the gear that I have never touched,
My father's stuff, bequeathed to be my prison,
With scrolls of vellum, blackened and besmutched,
Where still the desk-lamp's dismal smoke has risen.
Better have spent what little was my own,
Than sweat for petty gains by midnight oil.
The things that men inherit come alone
To true possession by the spirit's toil.
What can't be used is trash; what can, a prize
Begotten from the moment as it flies.
   But what magnetic thing compels my gaze?
This phial fascinates me, like the sight
Of soothing moon when, deep in forest ways,
Our very thoughts are silvered with the light.

    You I salute, you flask of virtue rare,
That now I hand me down with reverent care;
In you I honour human wit and art.
You very spirit of the opiate flowers,
You distillation of the deadly powers,
Show to your master now your gracious heart:
To see you, touch you, soothes my strife and pain.
I hear a call towards the open main,
My tide of soul is ebbing more and more,
Lies at my feet the shining, glassy plain,
A new day beckons to another shore.

    As if on wings, a chariot of fire
Draws near me. I am ready to be free.
Piercing the ether, new-born, I aspire
To rise to spheres of pure activity.
This soaring life, this bliss of godlike birth,
How shall we earn it, who from worms must rise?
Yet true the call: I spurn the sun of earth,
Leave, resolute, its loveliness. My eyes
I lift in daring to fling wide the gate
Whose threshold men have ever flinching trod.
The hour is come, as master of my fate
To prove in man the stature of a god,
Nor blench before the cavern black and fell,
Imagination's torment evermore,
But dare the narrow flaming pass of hell
And stride in strength towards the dreaded door.
This step I take in cheerful resolution,
Risk more than death, yea, dare my dissolution.

    Pure crystal bowl, I take you from your case,
Come down, to help me, from your waiting-place.
Long have I owned your worth with unconcern,
You who could charm, upon high holidays,

Night

My father's guests, and shining win their praise,
As each received the loving-cup in turn.
The pride of art, the legends in the frieze,
The drinker's pledge, to tell them all in rhyme,
Then lift the cup and drain it to the lees –
All brings me back the nights of youthful prime.
I shall not hand you now to any friend,
No witty praise of art do I intend,
For here's a cordial quick to drown the sense,
A chalice with dark opiate to dispense:
I choose, clear-eyed, the draught of my preparing
And drink my last, with all my spirit daring
To pledge the morrow's awful imminence.
      (*He sets the chalice to his lips.*
    There is a sound of bells and solemn choir.)

CHOIR OF ANGELS. Christ is risen!
  Joy to mortality,
  Men whom fatality
  Creeping, inherited,
  Deeply dispirited
  Doomed to a prison.

FAUST. What depth of chanting, whence the blissful tone
  That lames my lifting of the fatal glass?
  Do bells already tell with vibrant drone
  The solemn opening of the Easter Mass,
  And choirs with comfort's anthem now resume
  The angelic breaking of the darkened tomb,
  The token of a compact come to pass?

CHORUS OF WOMEN. With spices and balm
  Fain had we tended him,
  Laid him in calm,
  Faithful befriended him.
  Wraps had we wound,

> Pure linen laid on,
> Alas, and we found
> Our Saviour was gone.

CHORUS OF ANGELS. Christ is raised up,
> Death has no sting,
> Love's blessed King
> Lives conquering
> Trials that bring
> Misery's cup.

FAUST. Why seek ye, heavenly sounds so mild
> And mighty, me in dust distressed?
> Go sing where tender souls are domiciled.
> I hear, but lack the faith, am dispossessed;
> And faith has wonder for its dearest child.
> This is a sphere to which I may not venture,
> This source of things sublime, this lofty strain;
> And yet the sound brings back my soul's indenture
> Of early years, calls me to life again.
> Time was, with sweetest touch dear heaven's kiss
> Would light upon me in the sabbath stillness.
> Then had the bells a sound of boding fulness
> And every prayer was ecstasy of bliss.
> A strangely lovely fervency, a yearning
> Drove me to stray in fields and forests far,
> And when my heart was loosed, and tears came burning,
> I neared the threshold where no sorrows are.
> This melody the bliss of childhood taught me,
> The song of innocence, the joy of spring;
> And thoughts of youth, this solemn hour, have brought me
> In my last step a childlike wavering.
> Begin once more, O sweet celestial strain.
> Tears dim my eyes: earth's child I am again.

CHORUS OF THE DISCIPLES. He in the tomb who lay
  Now is ascended,
  Glorious reached the day,
  Where death is ended.
  Blissfully grows he near
  To his creative power;
  Still must we sojourn here,
  Biding our earthy hour.
  Left he us all, his own,
  Languishing here like this;
  Ah, we do but bemoan,
  Master, thy bliss.
CHORUS OF ANGELS. Christ is arisen
  From foulness of death's decree.
  Lo, from your prison,
  Love sets you free.
  Prize him and praise:
  In witness always,
  At bread when you raise
  Your brotherly lays.
  Who works and who prays,
  As love fills his days,
  May know without fear
  His master is near.

OUTSIDE THE CITY GATE

(People of all sorts are going out walking.)

SOME APPRENTICES.
  Why do you think that way's the best?
OTHERS. We're for the huntsman's hostel up the hill.
FIRST SPEAKERS. But we were making for the mill.
AN APPRENTICE. I vote we go to Ferry Hatch.

ANOTHER. That's not much catch.
OTHERS. What about you?
A THIRD.   I'm going with the rest.
A FOURTH.
  At Castle Inn there's beer that's worth the climb,
  And wenches who will give you a good time,
  And pretty cudgel-play, you'll find.
A FIFTH. A pretty lad you are, upon my word,
  Twice on the loose, and itching for a third.
  The very place is sickening, to my mind.
A SERVANT-GIRL.
  Oh no, I'm going home. I shall not stay.
OTHERS. We're sure to find him by the poplar-trees.
FIRST GIRL. That doesn't make me happy, anyway,
  It's you he walks with, you he seeks to please;
  You dance with him for everyone to see,
  What's happiness of yours to do with me?
OTHERS. He won't be by himself: to-day, he said,
  He'd bring with him for sure the curly-head.
STUDENT. Gad, how those buxom lasses stride along!
  Come, brother, this is where we can't go wrong:
  A pipe of shag, a glass of barley-wine,
  And then a well-dressed wench will suit me fine.
CITIZEN'S DAUGHTER.
  Just look, that fair boy, with his fellow-student,
  A scandal, nothing less, I tell you flat:
  They're fellows fit for girls refined and prudent,
  And then they chase a pair of sluts like that!
SECOND STUDENT (*to the first*).
  Don't rush, there's two behind us, man, go slower,
  In pretty dresses with a touch of class;
  My neighbour's daughter's one, I'm sure I know her;
  I have, in fact, a soft spot for the lass.

They're coming on, both proper and demure,
But in the end they'll go with us, for sure.
FIRST STUDENT.
Good brother, no. I hate these coy addresses.
Come on, before we let our pheasants fly.
The hand that has the week-day broom to ply,
On Sunday gives the pleasantest caresses.
CITIZEN. No, Sir, the new-elected mayor's no good,
And, now he's in, grows worse: I said he would.
And what's he doing for the city, pray?
Daily the fortunes of the place decline,
While we must more than ever toe the line;
But one thing's sure: there's always more to pay.
A BEGGAR (*singing*). Kind sirs and ladies, passing by,
With cheeks so bright and clothes so pretty,
Pray see, how wretchedly I lie,
And spare me help as well as pity.
Let me not sing in vain and play!
Who gives, has joy within his keeping.
When all are glad on holiday,
Be that for me a time of reaping.
ANOTHER CITIZEN.
When Sunday comes, or times of holiday,
Let's talk of fights: there's nothing I like more
Than news of Turkey, or lands far away,
Where malcontents have loosed the dogs of war.
You stand at windows, with your drop of drink,
And watch the river's coloured traffic gliding,
And then, when evening comes, go home and think
How good it is to live in peace abiding.
THIRD CITIZEN.
Good neighbour, that's the view I take, egad!
They're free to break their heads across, I say;

Let all the world go topsy-turvy mad,
But here we keep secure the same old way.
OLD WOMAN (*to Citizen's Daughters*).
Hey, dressed so fine! young blood, in pretty fillies!
For you what gallant wouldn't be on fire?
No hoity-toity! – I know what your will is,
And I have means to get you your desire.
CITIZEN'S DAUGHTER.
Quick, Agatha, of such a witch keep clear;
In public you'll avoid her, if you're wise.
On Andrew's Eve she summoned up, my dear,
My future lover, right before my eyes.
SECOND CITIZEN'S DAUGHTER.
She showed me mine, within a crystal sphere,
A soldier-boy, with other men of daring.
I look around, I seek him far and near,
But never find him, and am nigh despairing.
SOLDIERS. Citadels high,
Fortifications,
Girls that deny
Love's invitations
With pride in their eyes,
To bring to submission
Is my ambition.
Bold the endeavour
And handsome the prize.
  Trumpets may bray,
Bidding the brave
Let come what may,
Joy or the grave.
A gay life and short!
On, to the field!
Maiden or fort,

Make 'em both yield.
Bold the endeavour,
Handsomely won.
Paid is the soldier,
Then he is gone.
    (Faust and Wagner enter.)
FAUST. Freed from the ice the brooklet flows,
 Touched by the Spring's life-giving glances.
River and stream forget the snows,
Hopeful the valley's green advances.
Decrepit winter halting goes
Back to his savage mountain ranges;
There, still retreating, weaker grows,
And grainy shuddering fingers strows –
Impotent ice on April's changes.
Before the sun the white is sped,
He sets astir with growth and springing
The world of colour he is bringing;
But, since the flowers lie dark within their bed,
He makes the dressed-up mortals serve instead.
Turn and look back, see from this height
The city lying in the light.
From the black cavernous outer gate
Come motley multitudes in spate.
In sunshine will they walk abroad
To keep the Raising of the Lord,
For they themselves are resurrected
From hovels and oppressive rooms
And ugly walls and garret glooms,
And trades and guilds where they're subjected.
From streets that stifle, crowds that crush,
From the dark church's cloistered hush,
They all come tumbling to the light.

See, how the fields and crofts invite
The lively mob to force its way;
And how the river bears its boats
Upon its bosom broad and gay,
Where swim the dancing craft, and floats
The last full-laden barge away.
Even the distant mountain track
Signals its spots of colour back.
At hand I hear the village wake,
Loud with the jollity they make,
Here young and old rejoice in deep content:
Here I am man, and claim man's element.

WAGNER. To walk with you, Sir, I rejoice,
I'm honoured and I'm edified,
But, frankly, this would hardly be my choice,
For such vulgarity I can't abide.
This shouting, fiddle-scraping, skittle-banging,
To me is all cacophonous and wrong;
They roar like things of Satan's hellish clanging,
And then they call it pleasure, call it song.

(Peasants under the lime-tree, with song and dance.)

SINGER. The shepherd donned his Sunday-best,
   With ribboned coat and flowered vest,
     A-dancing would he go.
   'Twas crowded underneath the lime,
   They danced like mad, in whirling time,
CHORUS. And diddle-dee,
     Hi-diddle-dee,
     So went the fiddle bow.
SINGER. And quick he joined the dancers' whirl
   And bumped into a pretty girl,
     The sturdy shepherd-beau.
   The lively wench, she turned around

    And called him 'clumsy lad' and frowned,
CHORUS. And diddle-dee,
      Hi-diddle-dee,
    To treat a poor girl so!
SINGER. But now the rout had reached its height,
    They danced to left, they danced to right,
      They swung with skirts a-flying.
    And red they grew and very warm,
    And staid for breath, still arm-in-arm,
CHORUS. And diddle-dee,
      Hi-diddle-dee,
    Elbow on hip was lying.
SINGER. 'Now don't behave as though I'm yours,
    A man says often he adores,
      And lies, as maidens know.'
    And yet he coaxed her on the sly,
    While from the limes resounded high
CHORUS. The diddle-dee,
      Hi-diddle-dee,
    With shout and fiddle-bow.

AN OLD PEASANT.
    Your Honour's good to walk our way:
    We see, and take it kindly, Sir,
    That you, so learned, can prefer
    To join with us on holiday.
    Then take this tankard, Doctor, pray,
    Our best, well filled with choicest draught:
    To you refreshed may Heaven give,
    For every drop that you have quaffed,
    An added happy day to live.
FAUST. I take the cup of cheer you kindly give,
    And thank you all, and wish you long to live.
        (*The people gather round in a ring.*)

OLD PEASANT. 'Tis well bethought, you come to-day,
   When all are happy and content,
For, Doctor, you were true to us
   In days of evil and lament.
And many a one stands here alive
   Whom your dear father's excellence
Plucked from the fever's fearful grip,
   Making an end to pestilence.
And you, a young man in those days,
   Took every plague-house in your round;
They bore the corpses out, but you
   Came from those places safe and sound,
Endured what men are tested by,
Our help below, helped from on high.
ALL. To him, preserved, good health, good will!
   And may he live to help us still!
FAUST. Nay, bow yourselves to him above,
   Who helps and teaches in his love.
        (*He passes, with Wagner, on his way.*)
WAGNER. What feelings, Sir, your heart must realize,
   To see the tribute of the wondering crowd!
Happy the man commanding such a prize
   By gifts with which his genius is endowed!
The father shows you to his little son,
And where you walk the people stand and stare,
The eager wonder seizes everyone,
The fiddler pauses and the dance is done,
And people cheer, and hats fly in the air.
A little more, and down they'd kneel, almost
As if the priest had raised the sacred Host.
FAUST. Not far above us lies that ledge of stone,
   Our quietest rest from walking will be there.
Here, pensive, I have often sat alone,

And searched my heart in fasting and in prayer.
So rich in hope, of lofty faith possessed,
With sighs and tears and wringing of my hands,
I thought to force from heaven's high commands
The termination of the raging pest.
And now this praise means mockery and blame.
If only you could read within my soul,
How little sire or son can truly claim
The virtues that these simple folk extol!
My father worked with honour none too clear,
Poring on Nature and her dark dominion,
An ardent scholar, with a mind sincere,
Yet crossed with cranks and obstinate opinion.
In company of choice practitioners
He tended cauldrons of the midnight crew.
From countless secret recipes these sirs
Concocted fearful things of foulest brew.
Then a red lion, eager his love to claim,
Was mated to the lily, warmly brewed,*
And both, subjected to the open flame,
From bridal to fresh bridal-bower pursued.
They thereupon, in dazzling hues, descried
The queen of beauty, in their glass immured.
That was the physic! True, their patients died,
But no-one ever asked them who was cured.
So, with a nostrum of this hellish sort,
We made these hills and valleys our resort,
And ravaged there more deadly than the pest.
These hands have ministered the deadly bane
To thousands who have perished; I remain
To hear cool murderers extolled and bless'd.

WAGNER. But why should you, Sir, rack your mind?

* Chemical terms—See Introduction, p. 16.

Surely a worthy man does well
Who can with diligence excel
In arts tradition has assigned.
You owed your father, Sir, compliance,
And honoured what he taught your youth;
If in your prime you further science,
Your son may reach an even higher truth.

FAUST. Ah, happy he who still can hope to rise,
Emerging from this sea of fear and doubt!
What no man knows, alone could make us wise;
And what we know, we well could do without.
But let not mortal troubles cast their shades,
Before this hour of sweet content has run.
Mark, now, the glimmering in the leafy glades,
Of dwellings gilded by the setting sun.
Now slants the fiery god towards the west,
Hasting away, but seeking in his round
New life afar: I long to join his quest,
On tireless wings uplifted from the ground.
Then should I see, in deathless evening-light,
The world in cradled stillness at my feet,
Each valley hushed, fire touching every height,
While silver brooks in golden rivers meet.
Then mountains could not check my god-like flight,
With wild ravine or savage rocky ways;
But lo, the sea, with warm and tranquil bays,
Would hold its beauty to my wondering sight.
And now at length the sun-god seems to sink,
Yet stirs my heart with new-awakened might,
The streams of quenchless light I long to drink,
Before me day and, far behind, the night,
The heavens above me, and the waves below:
A lovely dream, but gone with set of sun.

Ah me, the pinions by the spirit won
Bring us no flight that mortal clay can know.
And yet an inborn impulse bids us rise,
As with an aspiration, constant, strong,
When, lost from sight in blue and dazzling skies,
The skylark scatters thrilling shafts of song,
Or when, above the pines and mountain trees,
The eagles wide of pinion veer and sway,
And far across the open plains and seas
The stately cranes will wing their homeward way.

WAGNER. I've times myself when fancies fill my mind,
But not with any longing of that kind.
We soon grow sick of seeing woods and fields.
I never envy birds their wings. My need
Is all for books, from page to page to read.
Ah, what a different joy sweet study yields!
Then winter nights are glad, though winds may whistle,
Then limbs are warmed, as with a blissful mirth,
For when we spread a precious scroll or missal,
The joy of heaven itself comes down to earth.

FAUST. By this one passion you are quite possessed –
You'd best admit no other to a share.
Two souls, alas, are housed within my breast,
And each will wrestle for the mastery there.
The one has passion's craving crude for love,
And hugs a world where sweet the senses rage;
The other longs for pastures fair above,
Leaving the murk for lofty heritage.
O spirits, if there be, that range the air,
Swaying in potency 'twixt heaven and earth,
Come down, from out your golden skyey lair,
Bear me to beauteous life, another birth.
Yea, if a cloak of magic could be mine,

With power to bear me far in foreign lands,
I would not change it for the raiment fine
Of monarch throned with royal star and bands.

WAGNER. Nay, call not on the well-known fatal horde,
That floats and spreads upon the twilight arc,
To loose their store of evil things abroad,
And brew mankind a thousand dangers dark.
Then from the north the sharp-toothed spirits fly,
And plague and pierce you with their arrowy tongues;
Or from the east they swarm and parch you dry
And feed upon your lungs.
When noon-day sends the desert's flaming pest
With fierce and fiercer brunt to beat the brain,
Refreshing hosts give promise from the west,
Only to drown with deluge field and plain.
These sprites have ready ears, on evil bent,
Pretend obedience, planning to defeat us,
Assume the form of things from heaven sent
And lisp with angel tongues their lies to cheat us.
But let us go: the grey of evening falls,
The air is chilled, the creeping mists arise.
Dusk is the hour when homely firelight calls.
Why stay you, Sir, and gaze with earnest eyes?
What sight can grip you in the eventide?

FAUST. D'you see a jet-black dog now scampering wide
Through corn and stubble?

WAGNER.   Him I have espied
Some time ago, but gave him not a thought.

FAUST. Look closer now, with care, and say what sort
Of beast you think he is.

WAGNER.   Why, Sir, a hound
Of poodle breed, who snuffs his way around
To find his master.

FAUST.   Mark the spiral trail
  With which he comes from far, yet ever nigher
  Encircling us: unless my senses fail
  His track is traced with little tongues of fire.
WAGNER. Some optical illusion, Sir, maybe:
  He's nothing but a poodle-dog to me.
FAUST. It seems like magic tracing of a snare,
  Or meshes in our future pathway spread.
WAGNER. I'm sure he seeks his master everywhere,
  And frets to find two strangers here instead.
FAUST. The circle narrows, brings him near.
WAGNER. A dog, Sir – see, no phantom have we here!
  He growls, misdoubts, and settles on his hocks,
  And wags his tail: all canine orthodox.
FAUST. Come here then, sirrah, come with us!
WAGNER. The animal has all the poodle's fuss,
  For if you stop he stays expectant, too;
  You speak, and he'll come jumping up at you.
  Try him: he'll know the good retriever's trick,
  Or dash into the water for your stick.
FAUST. Friend, you are right: this cunning quaint result
  Is due to training, nothing here occult!
WAGNER. A dog that hears his trainer, and complies,
  Can win affection even from the wise.
  And this one earns your grace with his discerning:
  He, scholar-like, looks up to men of learning.
           (They enter the gate of the town.)

FAUST'S STUDY (ii)

(Faust enters, followed by the poodle.)

FAUST. Behind me lie the fields and brakes,
All dark beneath the starry pole,
And now with holy dread there wakes
The pure awareness of the soul.
From wild desire she rises free,
And sweetness dwells where passion trod.
Now to the heart speaks charity,
And in the heart the love of God.

O sirrah, down! Why snuffle at the door?
You restless dog, here's not the place to rove.
My cushion – there! Don't wander any more
As if you're lost: lie down behind the stove.
Out there you showed a poodle's pedigree,
And played your tricks upon the hilly crest;
But if I give you hospitality,
Lie down, and be my welcome quiet guest.

Within this little room again
The lamp burns peacefully and kind,
And light has steady, soft domain
Upon my bosom and my mind.
The heart comes to itself, and clear
The voice of hope and reason speaks,
Again the wells of life grow dear,
Whose water-springs our spirit seeks.

Cease growling, sir! That puppy sound
Comes jarring on the hallowed tone
With which my soul would dwell alone.
True, human beings may abound

Who growl at things beyond their ken,
Mocking the beautiful and good,
And all they haven't understood:
Let dogs not join these gentlemen.

    Ay me, though humbly I entreat for rest,
No more comes sweet contentment to my breast.
Must we then find so soon the fountain dry,
And man in thirsty torment left to lie?
That is the truth that long experience brings,
Yet may these sorrows bear a compensation:
We learn to cherish here immortal things,
And look with longing hearts for revelation,
Whose high inspired and wonder-bearing word
Most clear in the New Testament is heard.
My mind is moved this hour to consecrate,
In simple, honest will to understand
The sacred codex, and its truth translate
In the loved accents of my native land.

    (He opens a volume and sets to work.)
'Tis writ, 'In the beginning was the Word.'
I pause, to wonder what is here inferred.
The Word I cannot set supremely high:
A new translation I will try.
I read, if by the spirit I am taught,
This sense: 'In the beginning was the Thought.'
This opening I need to weigh again,
Or sense may suffer from a hasty pen.
Does Thought create, and work, and rule the hour?
'Twere best: 'In the beginning was the Power.'
Yet, while the pen is urged with willing fingers,
A sense of doubt and hesitancy lingers.
The spirit comes to guide me in my need,
I write, 'In the beginning was the Deed.'

If in my room you wish to share,
Stop whining, poodle, and forbear
Your yelps. I pray you, cease!
You thoroughly destroy my peace.
I can't have such a comrade near me,
One of us two must go, I fear me.
As host, I am reluctant to withdraw;
But you are free, good poodle, there's the door!
Yet – what must my eyes behold!
Has nature such enigmas to unfold?
The dog assumes a stature strange to see:*
Is it a phantom, or reality?
He rises up in might,
No canine form has such a height.
What spectre have I harboured here,
That like a hippopotamus comes near,
With fearful fangs and fiery, staring brow?
Nay, but I have you now!
For such a hybrid brood of hell,
The Key of Solomon will serve me well.†

SPECTRES (*in the cloisters*).

Pinned and trapped within is one:
Stay without, let follow none!
Like a fox, in cage or snare,
Hell's old lynx is quaking there.
But take heed!
Hover, hover, high and low,
To and fro,
Soon, with care, we'll have him freed.
Spirits, lend your cunning aid,

---

* See Introduction, p. 23.

† *Clavicula Salomonis*, a venerable book of magic, originally in Hebrew, for the domination of hellish apparitions.

Leave him not in irons dismayed,
He served us much, we are his debtors,
And now must save him from his fetters.
FAUST. First, to confront this thing of hell,
I must repeat the four-fold spell:
Salamander bright shall burn,
Sylph invisible shall turn,
Undine flow within her wave,
Kobold shall slave.
They who ignore
Recondite lore
Of elements' force,
Their nature and course,
Never will quell
Spirits of hell.
Vanish in the flames of fire,
Salamander!
Shine amid the starry choir,
Sylphide!
Swirl upon the streaming strand,
Undine!
Bring the homely helping hand,
Incubus, Incubus!
Come, stand forth, at my command!
None of the elemental four
Stirs in the beast, but as before
He grins, untroubled, from the floor,
Untouched by stroke of magic lore.
Shall hear me still,
Subjected by my will.
If that you be
Hell's progeny,
Look on this sign,

    Symbol divine,
    And, Satan-brood, bow!
Ah, how he looms and bristles now!
    What recognition,
    Thing of perdition,
    Strikes on your vision accurst?
    See you the infinite,
    Increate, permanent,
    Soul unpronounceable
    Stream in the firmament?
    Him whom they wantonly pierced?
Cowering from the spell,
Still he seems to loom and swell.
Like a behemoth of shade,
From the stove he would invade
All the room in frightful cloud,
Up to the roof. So, down, you proud
Spawn of hell! Lie at my feet!
The power I wield is no deceit:
I'll wither you with sacred flame.
Wait not the ray
That pierces, burning, from the trinal name!
Wait not, I say,
My incantation in its fullest measure!

MEPHISTOPHELES (*as the mist subsides, he comes forward from behind the stove, in the dress of a travelling scholar*).
Why all this noise? What is your worship's pleasure?

FAUST. So, that is then the essence of the brute!
A travelling scholar? Time for laughter yet!

MEPHISTOPHELES. I give your learned worship my salute,
And own, you put me in a pretty sweat.

FAUST. What is your name?

MEPHISTOPHELES.   Small, Sir, the question seems

From one who gives the Word its lowest rate,
Who, far removed from semblances and dreams,
Only the depths of life will contemplate.
FAUST. The nature of you doubtful gentlemen
Nomenclature may help to recognize,
As may be seen specifically when
We say Destroyer, Prince of Flies, or Lies.
Who then are you?
MEPHISTOPHELES. Part of a power that would
Alone work evil, but engenders good.
FAUST. What hidden meaning in this riddle lies?
MEPHISTOPHELES. The spirit I, that endlessly denies.
And rightly, too; for all that comes to birth
Is fit for overthrow, as nothing worth;
Wherefore the world were better sterilized;
Thus all that's here as Evil recognized
Is gain to me, and downfall, ruin, sin
The very element I prosper in.
FAUST. Part of a spirit you have claimed to be,
Yet stand before me whole.
MEPHISTOPHELES. In modesty
I state the simple truth. Let man's dim soul
Regard his toy-world as a perfect whole:
Part of a part am I, that once was all,
A part of darkness, mother of the light,
Proud light, that seeks a sway imperial,
Outranking far the ancient realm of night,
Yet strives in vain, doomed to be cleaving still
To forms embodied, struggle as he will.
He streams from matter, that he beautifies,
Yet matter gives him constant stubborn check;
Thus will he run, I trust, where ruin lies,
And so with matter share the general wreck.

FAUST. Why, now indeed your noble plan is plain:
  Your powers of grand annihilation fail,
  And so you traffic on a smaller scale.
MEPHISTOPHELES.
  And, frankly, even that brings little gain.
  Annihilation's forces meet resistance
  From something coarse asserting its existence.
  I toil away, endure through thick and thin,
  But never really get beneath its skin.
  Much earthquake, fire and flood have I applied,
  And still the placid sea and land abide.
  And then the cursèd brood of man and beast,
  What myriads have I buried of that spawn,
  And yet made no impression, not the least:
  Their blood will tingle fresh with every dawn.
  Thus on, and on! It drives one to despair!
  In elements of water, earth and air,
  In moisture or in drought, in warm or cold,
  A ceaseless multitude of seeds unfold.
  Flame is still mine, the power of flame alone,
  Else were there nothing I could call my own.
FAUST. And thus, against the ever-living
  Creative power, that heals us from our pain,
  You rage in your malevolent misgiving
  And clench the fist of treachery in vain.
  Strange, sterile son of Chaos, think anew,
  And find yourself some better thing to do.
MEPHISTOPHELES.
  The matters that you kindly mention
  Shall come up soon for our attention,
  But for the present, please, may I retire?
FAUST. I know you now, so why enquire?
  Come when you will: for self-effacement

Faust's Study

   Use, pray, the door; or here's the casement,
   Or travel by the flue above the fire.
MEPHISTOPHELES. I must admit, my exit from the scene
   Is discommoded by a trifling thing;
   The devil-charm above your door, I mean.
FAUST. You find my pentagram embarrassing?
   If that forbids you, tell
   How came you in, you child of hell?
   And how is such a spirit caught or cheated?
MEPHISTOPHELES.
   Beg pardon, Sir, the drawing's not completed,
   For here, this angle on the outer side
   Is left, you notice, open at the joint.
FAUST. Thus fortune sometimes scores a lucky point!
   It seems my prisoner you must abide,
   In proof that profit may arise from chance.
MEPHISTOPHELES.
   The poodle entered blindly in his prance,
   But now the thing assumes a serious shape:
   The devil's in the house with no escape.
FAUST. Why not the casement?
MEPHISTOPHELES.   By your leave,
   All fiends and phantoms must obey a law
   To use the way they entered in before.
   Thus are they free; else, thralled beyond reprieve.
FAUST. So hell has regulations to enact?
   Good, for with law a man can make a pact,
   Then why not with you gentlemen of hell?
MEPHISTOPHELES.
   What hell shall pledge, is yours to savour well,
   You shall not play to find the cards are stacked;
   But bonds like this aren't easy to achieve.
   I promise you, when space and time allow,

A further talk; but I entreat you now,
   Permit me, Sir, to take my humble leave.
FAUST. Yet stay a moment more: I long to learn
   Some tidings of the future's veiled event.
MEPHISTOPHELES.
   Nay, let me go! And soon I will return
   To bide your question to your heart's content.
FAUST. Not I it was who whistled you from hell;
   A self-willed bird, you flew upon the lime.
   Who holds the devil, let him hold him well,
   He hardly will be caught a second time.
MEPHISTOPHELES. If it so please you, I consent to stay,
   To bear you company, upon condition
   I use my arts to while the time away,
   In this I crave your worship's kind permission.
FAUST. I'll see your arts. You have my full consent,
   If what you have is pleasant to present.
MEPHISTOPHELES.
   This hour, my friend, shall stir your senses, more
   Than any pleasures you have known before,
   More than a year in tame existence spent.
   The things the dainty spirits sing you,
   Ay, and the lovely sights they bring you,
   Are something more than magic's empty show.
   Your palate shall be satisfied,
   Your sense of fragrance gratified,
   And all your subtle feelings set aglow.
   No need have I of paltry preparation.
   We are well met: begin the incantation.
SPIRITS. Lift the dull mantle
   Vaulted and darkling!
   Let the sweet blue,
   Brilliant, gentle,

Faust's Study

Swim to the view.
Living and sparkling
Azure will banish
Shades of the vaulting;
Cloud-wrack will vanish,
Tenderly halting
Stars will shine through.
Sunlight is seen
Softer in sheen.
From the four quarters,
Swaying and teeming,
Fair heaven's daughters
Bow with the gleaming
Beauty of dreaming
Over the waters;
And the heart's longing
Follows their thronging.
Clothed then in streaming
Ribands of heaven,
Lo, they are given
Beauty that covers
Many a bower,
Where the fond lovers
Pledge the soul's hour,
Covers the vernal
Springing eternal
Of the heart's flower.
Then from the vine
Tendrils will twine,
Grapes in their masses
Burden the presses,
Pour purple lustres
Crushed from their clusters.

Gushing in streams
Runs the rich wine,
Flowing where gleams
Amethyst shine,
Flowing by hills
Wooded, benign,
Leaving the rills
Incarnadine.
Then the winged throng
Taste in their flight
Joy and delight,
Floating along,
Upward and onward,
Where the sun smiles,
Winging for sunward
Fortunate isles,
Blissful and bright,
Cradled in light.
Comes to us ringing
Jubilant singing,
While on the sward
See we the dancing
Figures advancing
In sweet accord.
Free, debonair,
Some will then fare
Far on the heights,
Others will share
Swimmers' delights,
Or in their flights
Swing through the air.
All are ensuing
Beauty's renewing,

Faust's Study

    Seeking in space
    Stars that are giving
    Fulness of living,
    Sweetness and grace.
MEPHISTOPHELES.
    He sleeps. Well done, my boys, my dapper crew,
    You've lulled him to a drowsy rendezvous.
    Take for this concert, pray, my cordial thanks.
    A pretty man to bind the Lord of Hell!
    Sink him in dreams, bemuse him with your pranks,
    Submerged in seas where fancies sway and swell.
    And now to break the threshold's magic spell
    A tooth of brother rat would serve me well.
    No lengthy conjuration shall I need:
    I hear one rustle near, and he shall heed.
        The master of the rats and mice,
    Of flies and frogs and bugs and lice,
    Bids you come forth and fearless gnaw
    The sacred symbol at the door,
    In places smeared by him with oil –
    One skips already to the toil!
    Now quick to work! Your lord is caught
    At the far corner, where the point is wrought.
    Just one more bite, the thing's complete!
    Sweet dreams, my Faust, until again we meet.
FAUST (*awaking*).
    Am I thus cheated? Vanished thus, it seems,
    The splendid legions by the spirits shaped,
    My devil nothing but a thing of dreams,
    And only a poor poodle has escaped?

FAUST'S STUDY (iii)

Faust. Mephistopheles.

FAUST. A knock? Come in! Who troubles now my rest?
MEPHISTOPHELES. 'Tis I.
FAUST. Come in!
MEPHISTOPHELES. I wait a third request.
FAUST. Come in, then.
MEPHISTOPHELES. That's the welcome I desire!
  I hope our friendship ripens well:
  I come, your megrims to dispel,
  In likeness of a noble squire,
  My coat embroidered, gold on red,
  My cloak of heavy silk brocade,
  A feathered cap upon my head,
  And at my side a saucy blade.
  I recommend for you, in short,
  An outfit of a similar sort:
  With freedom such as gods may give,
  Discover what it means to live!
FAUST. The pain of life, that haunts our narrow way,
  I cannot shed with this or that attire.
  Too old am I to be content with play,
  Too young to live untroubled by desire.
  What comfort can the shallow world bestow?
  Renunciation! – Learn, man, to forgo!
  This is the lasting theme of themes,
  That soon or late will show its power,
  The tune that lurks in all our dreams,
  And the hoarse whisper of each hour.
  Yet, each new day I shudder when I wake
  With bitter tears to look upon the sun,

Faust's Study

Knowing that in the journey he will make
None of my longings will come true, not one;
To see the tendrils of my joys that start,
Cankered with doubts, the mind's self-conscious tares,
To feel creation stir a generous heart,
Only to fail before life's mocking cares.
And when soft night has shrouded all the west,
My anxious soul will beg her peace supreme;
But still I lie forsaken, for my rest
Is shattered by the wildness that I dream.
The god who dwells enthroned within my breast
Can stir my inner vision's deepest springs,
But he who binds my strength to his behest
Brings no command to sway external things.
Thus life has taught me, with its weary weight,
To long for death, and the dear light to hate.

MEPHISTOPHELES.
  Yet death's no welcome stranger at the gate!
FAUST. Happy the man, on whose heroic brow
  He binds the blood-stained wreath, the victor's palms;
  Or rapturous dancer, whom the fates allow
  To meet the call within his loved one's arms.
  Would I could know that lofty spirit's might,
  To sink my soul, entranced, in endless night.
MEPHISTOPHELES.
  Yet, at a midnight hour, the chance was wasted,
  When someone let a phial go untasted.
FAUST. By spying, your all-knowing wit is warmed?
MEPHISTOPHELES.
  Omniscient? No, not I; but well-informed.
FAUST. If from my soul's bewildering maze
  A sweet remembered echo drew me,
  If lingering trace of childhood's ways

Sent thrilling, cheating memory through me,
My curse on all that guides the soul,
With wiles and witchery surrounded,
And sets her in this dismal hole
With flashing flattery confounded.
My curse upon the high intent
With which the mind engirds itself;
Cursed be illusion's wilful elf
By whom our senses all are blent.
Accursed be cheating honour's lure,
The fame that time will disallow,
The sense of holding things secure,
As wife and child, or man and plough.
My curse on pride, that will invite
Emboldened acts for Mammon's treasure,
On Mammon's hand that sets aright
The softest couch for idle pleasure.
Curse on the fragrance of the grape,
Curse be on love's sweet festival,
And cursed be hope, and faith, her ape,
And cursed be patience most of all.

CHORUS OF SPIRITS (*invisible*). Woe and despair!
Now have you felled
A world of things fair,
Whose beauty, quelled,
Falls through the air.
Your hand has held
Powers that no spirits dare
To share.
Beauty is by a demi-god destroyed:
We, sorrowing, bear
The fragments to the endless void.
   Strong son of earth,

With power beyond your birth,
Rise in your might,
Build new delight,
Again make whole
The temple of your soul,
Fair house wherein
Splendours of sense accrue;
Rise and begin
The melody of life anew.

MEPHISTOPHELES. These all belong to me,
My pretty infantry.
Hear them commending,
Cunning and coy,
Quests never ending,
Action and joy.
Go from your solitude
Coursing the world, renewed.
There where the sense has bright
Ichor of sweet delight,
There they invite.

    Leave off this traffic with your groping grief,
That like a vulture feeds upon your mind;
No company so vile but brings relief,
And marks you for a man among mankind.
By this I don't suggest
We thrust you in among the common herd.
I'm not the grandest person or the best,
But if you care to take me at my word
And join with me, and make a common quest,
I'm very much at your disposal,
That's my proposal:
I'll make a pact with you,
Without ado,

> Find what you crave,
> And see you through,
> Your comrade and your slave.

FAUST. And what return am I required to make?

MEPHISTOPHELES.
> A question time can settle – why insist?

FAUST. Nay, nay, the devil is an egoist,
> The help he gives is not for Heaven's sake.
> State your conditions clearly, thus and thus:
> Such servants in the house are dangerous.

MEPHISTOPHELES. Then here below in service I'll abide,
> Fulfilling tirelessly your least decree,
> If when we meet upon the other side
> You undertake to do the same for me.

FAUST. The other side weighs little on my mind;
> Lay first this world in ruins, shattered, blind:
> That done, the new may rise its place to fill.
> From springs of earth my joys and pleasures start,
> Earth's sunlight sees the sorrows of my heart;
> If these are mine no more when I depart,
> The rest concerns me not: let come what will.
> This is a theme to which I close my ears,
> Whether hereafter we shall hate or love,
> Or whether we shall find in distant spheres
> A sense of things below or things above.

MEPHISTOPHELES.
> Now that's the very spirit for the venture.
> I'm with you straight, we'll draw up an indenture:
> I'll show you arts and joys, I'll give you more
> Than any mortal eye has seen before.

FAUST. And what, poor devil, pray, have you to give?
> When was a mortal soul in high endeavour
> Grasped by your kind, as your correlative?

Faust's Study

    Yours is the bread that satisfieth never,
    Red gold you have, dissolving without rest,
    Like quicksilver, to mock the gatherer's labour;
    The girl you give will nestle on my breast
    Only to ogle and invite my neighbour;
    Have you the game that only losers play,
    Have you the stars of honour that afflict
    With god-like dreams, only to fade away?
    Then show me fruits that rot before they're picked,
    Or trees that change their foliage every day.
MEPHISTOPHELES.
    A task that gives me little cause to shrink,
    I'll readily oblige you with such treasures.
    But now, my friend, the time is ripe, I think,
    For relishing in peace some tasty pleasures.
FAUST. If I be quieted with a bed of ease,
    Then let that moment be the end of me!
    If ever flattering lies of yours can please
    And soothe my soul to self-sufficiency,
    And make me one of pleasure's devotees,
    Then take my soul, for I desire to die:
    And that's a wager!
MEPHISTOPHELES.   Done!
FAUST.   And done again!
    If to the fleeting hour I say
    'Remain, so fair thou art, remain!'
    Then bind me with your fatal chain,
    For I will perish in that day.
    'Tis I for whom the bell shall toll,
    Then you are free, your service done.
    For me the clock shall fail, to ruin run,
    And timeless night descend upon my soul.
MEPHISTOPHELES. This shall be held in memory, beware!

FAUST. And rightly is my offer thus construed!
   What I propose, I do not lightly dare:
   While I abide, I live in servitude,
   And whether yours or whose, why should I care?
MEPHISTOPHELES.
   I'll wait on you to-night, when you partake
   Of college gaudy, where the doctors dine;
   Only – since life, or let's say death's at stake –
   I'll bring you, please, a couple of lines to sign.
FAUST.
   So, black and white you want? You've never heard,
   Good pedant, that a man may keep his word?
   Is't not enough, a word that I have spoken
   Threads all my days, for ever to remind me?
   By changing floods the world itself is broken,
   Yet you'll invent a little pledge to bind me?
   And yet the rule – or dream – must be maintained
   In hearts that cherish honour's edifice.
   Happy the man who keeps his faith unstained:
   No sacrifice will come to him amiss.
   A parchment, notwithstanding, signed and sealed,
   Is bogey fit to make the bravest yield.
   The word expires, in passing to the pen,
   And wax and sheepskin lord it over men.
   Then, evil spirit, say what is your will:
   Is't parchment, brass, or marble that you favour?
   And shall I write with stylus, quill, or graver?
   See what a choice I offer: take your pick!
MEPHISTOPHELES. No need to overheat your rhetoric,
   Exaggerating items in your pride,
   When any scrap of paper's just as good:
   For signature, we'll use a drop of blood.
FAUST. If this avails to make you satisfied,

Faust's Study

    I'll join you in your little mummer's trick.
MEPHISTOPHELES. Blood is a juice of quality most rare.
FAUST. Pray have no fear that I shall break this bond,
    Since all my strength is in the thing I swear,
    And its pursuit shall be my only care.
    Too high have I aspired, self-pleasing, fond,
    When truthfully my rank's no more than yours.
    The mighty Spirit spurned my weak despair,
    And Nature closed to me her sacred doors.
    My thread of thought is severed in despite,
    I sicken, long revolted at all learning;
    Then let us quench the pain of passion's burning
    In the soft depth of sensual delight.
    Now let your muffled mysteries emerge,
    Breed magic wonders naked to our glance,
    Now plunge we headlong in time's racing surge,
    Swung on the sliding wave of circumstance.
    Bring now the fruits of pain or pleasure forth,
    Sweet triumph's lure, or disappointment's wrath,
    A man's dynamic needs this restless urge.
MEPHISTOPHELES.
    Wealth shall be yours, beyond all fear or favour,
    Be pleased to take your pleasures on the wing,
    Voluptuous beauty taste in everything,
    And may you flourish on the joys you savour.
    Fall to, I say; but plunge, and don't be coy.
FAUST. Have you not heard? – I do not ask for joy.
    I take the way of turmoil's bitterest gain,
    Of love-sick hate, of quickening bought with pain.
    My heart, from learning's tyranny set free,
    Shall no more shun distress, but take its toll
    Of all the hazards of humanity,
    And nourish mortal sadness in my soul.

I'll sound the heights and depths that men can know,
Their very souls shall be with mine entwined,
I'll load my bosom with their weal and woe,
And share with them the shipwreck of mankind.

MEPHISTOPHELES.
Listen to me, who have through aeons flown,
And chewed this barren food from year to year:
No mortal, from the cradle to the bier,
Digests the bitter dough; a god alone
Can hold this sense of oneness. In a blaze
Of lasting light he sees a whole serene,
But us he leads in chequered, darkened ways,
While yours are broken days
With night between.

FAUST. And yet I am resolved.

MEPHISTOPHELES. Why then, well said!
And yet one fear will hardly be denied –
For time is short and art is long – I dread
Lest you should suffer from a doubtful guide.
Choose, Sir, a poet for companionship,
And let this gallant range the bounds of thought
And every noble branch of knowledge strip,
That admirable qualities be brought
To crown with glory your illustrious head:
The lion-heart,
The swiftness of the fleeting hind,
The fire of Italy, where passions dart,
The northerner's enduring mind.
Of secrets that he teaches, first shall be
To blend deceit with magnanimity,
And with the ardour of a passionate man
To fall in love, – according to a plan.
Would such a one served me! I'd soon install him,

Faust's Study

   And Mr Microcosmos I would call him.
FAUST. What then am I, suppose a hostile star
   Puts such a human crown beyond my reach,
   And mocks the bliss my senses so beseech?
MEPHISTOPHELES.
   You are, when all is done – just what you are.
   Put on the most elaborate curly wig,
   Mount learned stilts, to make yourself look big,
   You still will be the creature that you are.
FAUST. I know. In vain I gathered human treasure,
   And all that mortal spirit could digest:
   I come at last to recognize my measure,
   And know the sterile desert in my breast.
   I have not raised myself one poor degree,
   Nor stand I nearer to infinity.
MEPHISTOPHELES. My worthy Sir, you view affairs
   Like other people, I'm afraid;
   But we, more cunning in our cares,
   Must take our joys before they fade.
   What, man! Confound it, hands and feet
   And head and backside, all are yours;
   And what we take while life is sweet,
   Is that to be declared not ours?
   Six stallions, say, I can afford,
   Is not their strength my property?
   I tear along, a sporting lord,
   As if their legs belonged to me.
   Then up! Let meditation be,
   And stride out in the world with me!
   I tell you what: your groping theorist
   Is like a beast led round and round and round
   By evil spirits on a barren ground
   Near to the verdant pastures he has missed.

FAUST. Then say, how best begin?
MEPHISTOPHELES. Away, Sir, come!
  Why hug this learned martyrdom?
  We've more exciting plans to launch
  Than leading students by the nose;
  Leave that to neighbour Doctor Paunch!
  Is threshing straw the penance you propose?
  The richest items of your knowledge
  You cannot tell to lads in college –
  And straight I hear one, there, outside.
FAUST. No, no, my door is shut to him to-day!
MEPHISTOPHELES. He's waited long, to be denied:
  Poor lad, he can't go empty away.
  Give me your cap and gown, Sir, quick,
  I'll cut a dash in this array;
  And trust my wit to do the trick.
  A quarter of an hour is all I need,
  While you prepare to travel, with all speed.
        (*Exit Faust.*)
MEPHISTOPHELES (*in the long robes of Faust*).
  So, knowledge and fair reason you'll despise,
  The highest powers by which poor mortals rise.
  The Prince of Lies it is that edifies you,
  With all the flash of magic he supplies you.
  Now is he mine, without a saving clause,
  For fate has put a spirit in his breast
  That drives him madly on without a pause,
  And whose precipitate and rash behest
  O'erleaps the joys of earth and natural laws.
  Him will I lead a pretty dance
  Through ways of savage life bedraggled,
  Through stifling acts of insignificance.
  He'll find the bargain over which he haggled

Faust's Study

    Shall leave him dumb-struck, writhing, sticking fast;
    Before his lips shall float a rich repast,
    To mock insatiable appetite;
    In vain he'll cry for comfort in his plight;
    Whether or not he owns the devil's might,
    His doom of ruin is secured at last.
            (*Enter a Student.*)
STUDENT. Arrived but lately, Sir, I straight
    Present myself, a candidate
    To learn devotedly from one
    Whose fame through all the land has run.
MEPHISTOPHELES.
    I'm honoured by esteem so well expressed,
    But, Sir, you see one here like all the rest:
    Have you, perhaps, applied at other doors?
STUDENT. I seek good counsel, and I beg for yours.
    I come with strength of heart and courage, please,
    And well provided with professors' fees.
    My mother pleaded hard against my going;
    But now I hope for something worth the knowing.
MEPHISTOPHELES.
    Well done, you're now on learning's very track.
STUDENT. And yet, I've half a mind, Sir, to go back:
    The walled-in close, and gloomy college hall,
    Don't suit my mind or temperament at all.
    Here we are crowded, cramped for space,
    No trees or greenery in the place:
    I sit in halls of sapience
    Devoid of hearing, sight or sense.
MEPHISTOPHELES. That's just a matter of experience.
    A child perhaps denies the breast at first,
    Yet soon delights to slake its infant thirst;
    And thus each day will bring you greater zest

To draw on wisdom's most beneficent breast.
STUDENT. O that my head upon her bosom lay!
But how to find her? Show me, Sir, the way.
MEPHISTOPHELES. Tell me, before you ask my views,
What faculty you mean to choose.
STUDENT. My mind is set to know the worth
Of Nature's laws in heaven and earth,
Investigating each resource
Of science to my satisfaction.
MEPHISTOPHELES. A very right and proper course,
But guard your mind against distraction.
STUDENT. I'll work with all my heart and soul,
But still should like, I must admit,
On summer days a little stroll
With time to sun myself a bit.
MEPHISTOPHELES.
Waste not your time: time's flight is fabulous;
Yet method teaches you to save it; thus,
I counsel first the depths you plumb
Of our Collegium Logicum.
Its rigour will confine your mind
Like Inquisition boots, you'll find,
And teach it hence to walk with reason,
Smoothly trained to thoughts in season,
Not let it stray through thick and thin,
Like Jack-o'-Lantern without discipline.
Then shall you learn in studious days
That actions and spontaneous ways
Like eating, drinking, are not free,
But subject to the rule of three.
The web of thought, I'd have you know,
Is like a weaver's masterpiece:
The restless shuttles never cease,

The yarn invisibly runs to and fro,
A single treadle governs many a thread,
And at a stroke a thousand strands are wed.
And so philosophers step in
To weave a proof that things begin,
Past question, with an origin.
With first and second well rehearsed,
Our third and fourth can be deduced,
And if no second were, or first,
No third or fourth could be produced.
This method scholars praise, and keenly clutch;
As weavers, though, they don't amount to much.
To docket living things past any doubt
You cancel first the living spirit out:
The parts lie in the hollow of your hand,
You only lack the living link you banned.
This sweet self-irony, in learned thesis,
The chemists call *naturae encheiresis*.

STUDENT. Beg pardon, but I've scarcely understood.

MEPHISTOPHELES.
Try to improve, and soon I'll make it good;
You'll learn with sage obedience, by and by,
To systemize and then to classify.

STUDENT. O Sir, I feel so dazed at what you've said;
It goes round like a mill-wheel in my head.

MEPHISTOPHELES. Next, most important thing of all,
To metaphysics you must fall,
And see with deep discernment plain,
What things won't fit the human brain;
But, fit or not, why vex your head? —
You use a sounding phrase instead.
But first, Sir, you must persevere
In method, for a good half-year.

Five lectures are your daily plan –
And show yourself a punctual man.
For your professor, pray, prepare;
No paragraph, Sir, overlook!
And then you soon will be aware
He never deviates from the book.
But write it down, Sir, every bit,
As if the Holy Ghost dictated it.

STUDENT. A lesson, Sir, I need not to be shown
A second time: I read its worth aright,
For anything we have in black and white
Is ours to take away and call our own.

MEPHISTOPHELES.
But now to choose your faculty, my friend.

STUDENT. I doubt if I'd be happy taking Laws.

MEPHISTOPHELES. A hesitation that I comprehend.
Knowing the subject, I myself would pause.
They've statutes, clauses, rights, in such a smother
As spreads from place to place the legal taint,
And ties one generation to another
Worse than a slow inherited complaint.
Sense becomes nonsense, charity a nuisance,
And grandsons learn to curse the lawyers' usance.
To free-born rights, the laws by Nature taught,
These learned gentry never give a thought.

STUDENT. Hearing your words I hate the subject more.
How blest are students entering your door!
Perhaps theology has claims more strong?

MEPHISTOPHELES.
Sir, I should grieve to see you going wrong.
The aspirants who choose that learned field
May fail to see the pitfalls, oversure;
And zealotry has virus so concealed,

Faust's Study

It's hard to tell the poison from the cure!
So, stick to one professor all your days,
And swear by every word the Master says.
In short, you pin your faith on words, my friend,
Make words your safeguard, so that you ascend
To certainty's high temple in the end.
STUDENT. But, Sir, concede
That words must have some meaning underlying.
MEPHISTOPHELES. Why yes, agreed,
But never fear to find that mortifying,
For if your meaning's threatened with stagnation,
Then words come in, to save the situation:
They'll fight your battles well if you enlist 'em,
Or furnish you a universal system.
Thus words will serve us grandly for a creed,
Where every syllable is guaranteed.
STUDENT. Pray pardon my detaining you with questions,
And grant that one more topic I begin:
I ask your pregnant comments and suggestions
Suppose my choice should light on Medicine.
God knows, I view the subjects with dismay,
With three short years to fit the whole lot in.
A hint from you would help me feel my way.
MEPHISTOPHELES (*aside*).
I've had enough of this doctorial tone,
It's time Old Nick did something of his own.
(*Aloud.*) Ah, Medicine? – I see no hardship there:
You learn the world of men, Sir, at your ease,
Then, in the end, let small and great ones fare
As God may please.
To scour around for sciences is vain,
Since mortals only learn what mortals can;
But he who turns the moment to his gain,

He is the proper man.
And, since you seem of pleasing build,
A certain boldness is your due.
Thus, with self-confidence fulfilled,
You'll find that folk have confidence in you.
Learn how to handle women, that make sure,
Since all the aches and sighs that come to vex
The tender sex
The doctor knows one little place to cure.
A bedside manner sets their hearts at ease,
And then they're yours for treatment as you please.
A string of letters following your name
Assures them that you far surpass your peers,
And so you handle favours as fair game
That other men would have to stalk for years.
Learn the sweet touches to the pulse applied,
And then, with looks discreet but fiery-eyed,
You lay your hands about her little waist
To ascertain how tightly she is laced.

STUDENT.
Now that makes sense! How good, to see one's way!

MEPHISTOPHELES. All theory, my friend, is grey,
But green is life's glad golden tree.

STUDENT.
Oh, Sir, your words are like a dream to me.
Permit me, please, this visit to repeat,
To learn more thoroughly at wisdom's feet.

MEPHISTOPHELES.
What gifts I have are yours, Sir, to receive.

STUDENT.
I scarce can bring myself to take my leave.
One kindness undertake on my behalf:
Inscribe my book, Sir, with your autograph.

Faust's Study

MEPHISTOPHELES. With pleasure.
   (*He takes the book, writes in it, and hands it back.*)
STUDENT (*reading*). *Eritis sicut Deus, scientes bonum et malum.*
   (*He closes the book reverently, and ceremoniously takes his leave.*)
MEPHISTOPHELES (*alone*).
  Follow the adage of my cousin Snake.
  From dreams of god-like knowledge you will wake
  To fear, in which your very soul shall quake.
FAUST (*entering*). Whither away?
MEPHISTOPHELES.   By any route you please,
  To see both high and low, by lands or seas.
  With what delight, what profit fabulous
  You'll revel through the charming syllabus.
FAUST. Bearded and grey, I fear I lack
  The sprightliness I need for the attack;
  I have the gravest doubts of my success,
  Deficient as I am in fine address.
  In front of other folk I often quail,
  And through embarrassment am bound to fail.
MEPHISTOPHELES.
  You'll soon improve, my friend, have no misgiving;
  Once self-assured, you learn the art of living.
FAUST. What means of travelling do you intend?
  Where are your coach, your servants or your horses?
MEPHISTOPHELES.
  I only have to spread this cloak, my friend,
  To bear us both, at will, on airy courses.
  To questions of your luggage pay no heed,
  On this bold trip there's no such paltry need.
  A little jet of fire I have in store
  To lift us from the earth, with strength to soar.
  We'll mount the quicker, being light of gear;
  Congratulations on your new career!

AUERBACH'S CELLAR IN LEIPZIG

Drinking Party.

FROSCH. What, nobody for a drink?
  Dull as a ditch, this place is.
  Some of you seem to think
  There's virtue in pulling long faces.
  Call yourselves lit-up, gay?
  The pack of you's as bright as mouldy hay.
BRANDER. What about you? A first-class mouldy gent,
  With not a word of smut or devilment.
FROSCH (*empties a glass of wine over Brander's head*).
  There's for a pretty start then.
BRANDER.   Blast your eyes!
FROSCH. You asked for it: it can't be a surprise.
SIEBEL. Quarrelling over a jest?
  Send for the chucker-out!
  Sing, my lads, open your chest,
  Sing, swill, my lads, and shout!
  Hey, Holla, Ho!
ALTMAYER.   God's death, some cotton wool!
  He blasts my earholes like a bellowing bull.
SIEBEL. If a man sings
  Till the roof rings,
  Enough to shake the place on him,
  He's got a proper bass on him.
FROSCH. Hear, hear! Chuck fellows out who take offence!
  Ri-tooral-ay!
ALTMAYER. Ri-tooral-ooral-addy!
FROSCH. Our pipes are tuned, I vote that we commence.
  (*Sings.*) The Holy Roman Empire, lads,
  What keeps its carcase going?

Auerbach's Cellar in Leipzig

BRANDER. A sweaty song! It stinks of politics.
  A nasty song! Thank God in constant prayer
  The Roman Empire isn't your affair.
  I thank my stars, and think myself the wiser,
  That no-one calls me Chancellor or Kaiser.
  Yet every house must have its corner-stone,
  So let's elect a Pontiff of our own,
  And honour him and set the man on high –
  You know the qualities to choose him by.
FROSCH (*singing*). On high, sweet nightingale, arise,
  And bring my love a thousand amorous sighs!
SIEBEL.
  Love-songs are barred. Who cares about your flame?
FROSCH. I'll sing of love and kisses all the same:
  (*Sings.*) Lift the latch, in midnight here I wait,
  The latch, my dove, your sweetheart's at the gate.
  Now bolt the latch, and slip away at dawn.
SIEBEL.
  Sing on, and praise your true-love, while I yawn,
  For I've encountered her of whom you prate:
  I wish that dove a devil for a mate,
  Who'll leave her at a cross-road, nicely tousled,
  Or an old goat from Witches' Sabbath sousled,
  Who, when she murmurs her 'Good-night, my sweet',
  Will gallop off and answer with a bleat.
  You'll find a lad of flesh and blood too fine
  For such a jilt, and then the laugh is mine.
  From me she gets no tribute or refrains,
  Except the sort to break her window-panes.
BRANDER (*banging on the table*).
  Order, order! Listen to me awhile!
  You know my taste: always the proper style.
  There's lovers in our crew conjoint,

And standing orders now require
I sing them something to the point –
And you can bellow in the choir.
(*Sings.*) Once in a cellar lived a rat,
A glutton and sweet-toother,
He grew his little paunch as fat
As that of Doctor Luther.
But Cook laid poison for his drink,
Which cramped his world and made him think
That love consumed his vitals.

CHORUS. That love consumed his vitals.

BRANDER. He squirmed and scampered all he knew,
And drank at every puddle,
And scratched and gnawed the whole house through,
But still in fiery fuddle.
Then fell he in a fearful stew,
And leapt and winced as creatures do
When love consumes their vitals.

CHORUS. When love consumes their vitals.

BRANDER. In agony he came at last
By daylight in the kitchen,
Flopped on the hearth-stone panting fast,
And piteously twitchin'.
Then laughed the poisoner and said,
'He lies like mortals, nearly dead,
When love consumes their vitals.'

CHORUS. When love consumes their vitals.

SIEBEL. Fat rascals love that sort of game!
It seems to me a bloody shame,
To feed poor rats on poisoned lard.

BRANDER. So rats stand high in your regard?

ALTMAYER. Sir Peter Paunch, with baldy head,
Is one of those soft-hearted creatures;

Auerbach's Cellar in Leipzig

And when a swollen rat lies dead
He sees in him his own dear features.
(Faust and Mephistopheles enter.)

MEPHISTOPHELES.
I bring you first where you can see
Convivial society.
Observe how smoothly life can go its way,
When folk make all the week a holiday.
With scanty wit, yet wholly at their ease,
Like kittens given their own tail to tease,
They confidently take their little floor,
And, barring headaches from the night before,
Or lack of credit on the landlord's slate,
They live profoundly pleased with their estate.

BRANDER. Those two are travellers, coming from afar,
Their foreign fashion tells you what they are,
Arrived this very hour, Sir, I'll be bound.

FROSCH.
You're in the right: our Leipzig is renowned,
A little Paris, as a social draw.

SIEBEL. What sort of people do you take them for?

FROSCH. Leave it to me, for with a glass or two
I'll worm out any secrets, I'll be sworn;
I draw them out like infants' teeth, I do.
I have a notion these are nobly born:
They entered proudly, with a touch of scorn.

BRANDER. Quack-doctors, both of them, I'll lay a dollar.

ALTMAYER. Perhaps.

FROSCH. Just watch, how soon I sort them out.

MEPHISTOPHELES.
They never dream the devil is about,
Not even if he has them by the collar.

FAUST. Good evening, gentlemen.

SIEBEL. To you the same.
> (*Aside, with a glance at Mephistopheles.*)
> That fellow has one foot a little lame.

MEPHISTOPHELES.
> D'you mind, Sirs, if we join your little party?
> Society both elegant and hearty
> Is very welcome when the wine is poor.

ALTMAYER. You have fastidious taste, Sir, to be sure.

FROSCH. I take it you left Rippach fairly late,
> And called on Hansen for your evening meal?

MEPHISTOPHELES.
> To-day we passed him by, we couldn't wait,
> But chatted with him last time, quite a deal.
> He talked about his cousin, by the way,
> And gave us special greetings to convey.
> > (*He singles out Frosch for a bow.*)

ALTMAYER (*sotto voce*). So much for you.

SIEBEL.   Ay, faith, the man's all there.

FROSCH. You wait, I'll catch the fellow unaware.

MEPHISTOPHELES. Do I mistake, or did we hear
> Some singing, with a choir select?
> This vaulted roof must echo clear,
> With fine acoustical effect.

FROSCH. Are you a virtuoso, Sir, in song?

MEPHISTOPHELES.
> Oh no! My will, but not my art, is strong.

ALTMAYER. Give us a tune!

MEPHISTOPHELES.   As many as you please.

SIEBEL. But give us something with a new refrain.

MEPHISTOPHELES.
> That I can do: we've just returned from Spain,
> The lovely land of wine and melodies.
> (*Sings*). Once on a time there lived a King,

Auerbach's Cellar in Leipzig

    Who had a handsome flea; –
FROSCH. Hear that, my friends? D'you hear? A flea!
    A pretty guest for company!
MEPHISTOPHELES. Once on a time there lived a King
    Who had a handsome flea;
  Dearer to him than anything,
    Even his son, was he.
  To wait his royal pleasure
    The tailor then he bade:
  'Go make him clothes to measure,
    And breeches for the lad.'
BRANDER. Take care the measurements to check!
    And bid the tailor use his wit,
  For if he wants to save his neck
    He'd better make the breeches fit.
MEPHISTOPHELES. In silks the most expensive
    The younker now was dressed,
  With ornaments extensive,
    And ribbons on his breast.
  He held important stations
    As minister of state,
  And all his poor relations
    Were placed among the great.

  The court was then a scene, Sirs:
    The ladies and their knights,
  The Wardrobe and the Queen, Sirs,
    They all had plaguey bites,
  And weren't allowed to scratch 'em,
    Because of etiquette;
  But we can grab and catch 'em,
    And kill the little pet.
CHORUS (*with hullabaloo*). But we can grab and catch 'em,

And kill the little pet.
FROSCH. Bravo, Sir! That's the stuff for me!
SIEBEL. And put an end to every flea!
BRANDER. Nip with your nails, lads, crack 'em fine!
ALTMAYER. Here's to liberty: bring in the wine!
MEPHISTOPHELES.
   I'd drink a glass to liberty, my friend,
   If only local vintage weren't so bad.
SIEBEL. You'd best not air that notion here, egad!
MEPHISTOPHELES.
   Agreed; I fear the landlord to offend,
   Or I would offer every worthy guest
   From our own cellar something of the best.
SIEBEL. In that case, good, I'll say 'twas my request.
FROSCH. But give no nips; such samples, Sir, I hate:
   A real good glass-full we appreciate.
   For if it's my judicious word you ask,
   You have to fill my gullet for the task.
ALTMAYER (*sotto voce*).
   They come from Rheinland, I presume.
MEPHISTOPHELES. Give me a gimlet.
BRANDER.   What's that for?
   You surely haven't casks outside the door?
ALTMAYER.
   The landlord's tools are there, across the room.
MEPHISTOPHELES (*takes the gimlet*).
   (*To Frosch.*) Now say, what's yours? A sparkling wine
      perhaps?
FROSCH. How's this? – Have you varieties, good Sir?
MEPHISTOPHELES. I'll give you all whatever you prefer.
ALTMAYER (*to Frosch*).
   Aha, you soon begin to lick your chaps.
FROSCH. Well, if I have to choose, I'll call for Rhein:

Auerbach's Cellar in Leipzig

First in our Fatherland's good gift of wine.
MEPHISTOPHELES (*boring a hole in the table-edge, where Frosch is sitting*).
Fetch me some wax to make the spigots, quick!
ALTMAYER. It's nothing but a conjuring trick.
MEPHISTOPHELES (*to Brander*). And yours?
BRANDER.   Champagne, dear Sir, is mine,
And let it be a foaming, sparkling wine.
(*Mephistopheles bores; meanwhile one of them has made the wax spigots, and plugged them in.*)
BRANDER. One can't be always banning foreign stuff,
We have to look abroad for much that's fine:
A German hates a Frenchman sure enough,
But has a true affection for his wine.
SIEBEL (*as Mephistopheles comes towards his place at the table*).
Sour vintages I always shall pass by:
I much prefer the sweet wines to the dry.
MEPHISTOPHELES.
Just say the word, and you shall have Tokay.
ALTMAYER. Sirs, look me in the face and let's be frank:
Is this a foolery or a silly prank?
MEPHISTOPHELES.
Tut, tut. In such distinguished company
Unseemly joking would be out of place.
Therefore speak up, Sir, what's the wine to be,
And I'll endeavour then to please Your Grace.
ALTMAYER. I'm not particular, if that's the case.
(*The holes are now bored and the stoppers fixed.*)
MEPHISTOPHELES (*with curious gestures*).
Sweet grapes are on a wine-stock borne,
The he-goat has a branch of horn.
Wine comes from juice, the grape from wood,
The table yields us wine as good.

Deep Nature has her wonders still,
So draw the bungs and drink your fill.

ALL (*drawing the spigots and seeing the wines of their choice flowing into their glasses*).

O grand! In fountains! To it, with a will!

MEPHISTOPHELES.

My compliments! And don't let any spill.
(*They drink again and again.*)

SEVERAL (*singing*). Hell's Hottentots we are for wine,
And lap the liquor as it flows,
And happy as a hundred swine
We drink, and don't care if it snows.

MEPHISTOPHELES.

Now they're let loose, in democratic bliss.

FAUST. Come, let us go, I've had enough of this.

MEPHISTOPHELES. Why rush away?
For if you stay
A revelation shall you see
Of charming bestiality.
(*Siebel drinks recklessly and spills the wine on the floor, where it bursts into flame.*)

ALL. Help! Fire! Give help! A hellish flame!

MEPHISTOPHELES.

Peace, friendly Element, be quiet and tame.
(*To the drinkers.*) A spot of purging fire, in wisdom's name.

SIEBEL. We'll make you sorry for it, all the same:
Who d'you take us for, man? What's your game?

FROSCH. I'll stop his jokes, no matter what he says.

ALTMAYER. And see him quietly off the premises.

SIEBEL. Come, come! How dare you, Sir, begin
Your hocus-pocus in our inn?

MEPHISTOPHELES. Silence, old beer-can!

SIEBEL. Broomstick, this to me!
  Will you add insult, Sir, to injury?
BRANDER. He's asking for it! Watch the fighting start!
ALTMAYER (*draws a plug from the table and receives a spurt of fire*). Fire, fire!
SIEBEL. Stab me this outlaw, practising black art!
  He's anybody's game! Strike for the heart!
  (*They draw their knives and advance upon Mephistopheles.*)
MEPHISTOPHELES (*with solemn gestures*).
  Mirage mount on sight and word,
  Vision, sense and place be blurred,
  And minds be distantly transferred.
    (*They stand and look at each other amazed.*)
ALTMAYER.
  Where may I be? And what this lovely land?
FROSCH. And vineyards!
SIEBEL. Ay, and clustering grapes to hand
BRANDER. And here beneath the roof of green
  The richly loaded stems are seen.
    (*He takes Siebel by the nose; the rest treat each other the same, and all raise their knives.*)
MEPHISTOPHELES (*solemnly, as before*).
  Illusion take your scales from off their eyes:
  The Devil's humour let them recognize!
    (*He vanishes with Faust. The drinkers let go of each other.*)
SIEBEL. What's this?
ALTMAYER. Ay, what?
FROSCH. I think I held your nose.
BRANDER. And I had hold of Siebel's, I suppose.
ALTMAYER.
  A sort of shock, it was, through every limb.
  Give me a chair, my head begins to swim.
FROSCH. But tell me, what's the meaning of it all?

SIEBEL. Where is the knave? If I could hold him fast,
  He'd realize that moment was his last.
ALTMAYER. I think I saw him hurtle through the hall
  Upon a barrel, riding in the air –
  My feet are leaden, bound,
    And dragging on the ground – (*Turning to the table.*)
  What if the wine's still flowing there?
SIEBEL. All lies it was, a phantom and a cheat.
FROSCH. And yet it seemed like wine, and tasted sweet.
BRANDER. And what about the clusters overhead?
ALTMAYER. And who will say that miracles are dead?

WITCH'S KITCHEN

On a low hearth a large cauldron hangs over the fire. In the fumes that rise up from it are seen several strange figures. A female monkey is sitting beside the cauldron, to skim it and see that it does not boil over. The male monkey, with the young ones, sits by, and warms himself. Walls and ceiling are hung with the fantastic furniture of witchcraft.

Faust enters, with Mephistopheles.

FAUST. This witch's quackery disgusts my soul!
  Is this your promise then, that I be healed
  By crooked counsel in this crazy hole,
  By truth in some decrepit dame revealed?
  Or will my age be thirty summers less
  By watching witches stir their scummy mess?
  Is this, alas, the summit and the force
  Of all your cunning? Was my hope so blind?
  Can Nature yield no salve or secret source,
  As fit requital for a noble mind?

Witch's Kitchen

MEPHISTOPHELES.
> My friend, you show the sense for which I look.
> There is, indeed, a recipe for youth,
> But that is hidden in another book,
> Writ in a chapter of the rarest truth.

FAUST. Then tell me!

MEPHISTOPHELES. Good. Here's Nature's recipe,
> Without a doctor, gold, or sorcery:
> Begin at once a life of open air,
> To dig and trench and cultivate the ground,
> Content yourself within the common round,
> And for your dinner have the homeliest fare.
> Live with the beasts, on equal terms; be sure
> That, where you reap, your hands must spread the dung.
> And there, my friend, you have the certain cure,
> By which at eighty years you still are young.

FAUST. All that to me is foreign: I'm afraid
> I lack ability to ply the spade,
> I've nothing with the simple life akin.

MEPHISTOPHELES. That's where the witch comes in.

FAUST. Still havering about the wretched crone!
> Cannot you brew an ichor of your own?

MEPHISTOPHELES.
> A pretty pastime! Meanwhile I postpone
> A thousand projects ardently desired?
> This needs not arts and sciences alone:
> A time of patient brooding is required.
> A subtle sprite can watch the brew for long,
> But only time can make the ferment strong.
> You scarce can guess the things the mixture needs,
> Ingredients passing strange are used to make it.
> From devil's teaching, true, the task proceeds,

And yet the Devil cannot undertake it.
(*Looking at the beasts.*)
Behold, the staff, a nice four-footed race!
The footman and the maid sit face to face.
(*To the animals.*) Your dame, it seems, is not at home?

THE ANIMALS. In a carouse,
Out of the house,
Up through the chimney
She has clomb.

MEPHISTOPHELES.
How long does she go roaming out of doors?

THE ANIMALS. Long enough for us to warm our paws.

MEPHISTOPHELES.
What's your impression of the dainty pair?

FAUST. Revolting beasts, unequalled anywhere.

MEPHISTOPHELES.
I disagree, for discourse of this kind
Has qualities exactly to my mind.
(*To the animals.*) Accursed minions – you, my jewel –
What is the brew your ladle stirs?

THE ANIMALS. We're cooking beggars' skilly-gruel.

MEPHISTOPHELES. With half the world for customers.

MALE MONKEY (*coming up to Mephistopheles with fawning*).
Just throw the dice,
That shall suffice
To make me wealthy.
Life isn't healthy,
But, given gold,
I'd be consoled,
Sober and nice.

MEPHISTOPHELES.
How happy would the greedy monkey be
To live on gambling or on lottery!

Witch's Kitchen

(*The young monkeys have meanwhile been playing with a large globe, which they now roll forward.*)

MALE MONKEY. The world, behold,
Is thus for ever rolled,
With ceaseless up and down,
And lo, its hollow crown
Resounds like glass,
Most apt to break, alas.
And here it gleams,
Here brighter seems.
True, that I live;
But see you give
Heed, my good son,
Or your days are done.
This sphere of clay
Will splinter on a day.

MEPHISTOPHELES. What purpose has this sieve?

MALE MONKEY (*reaching it down*). The sieve will show
If you're a thief or no.
(*He runs to the female monkey and makes her look through it.*)
Look through the sieve!
Ask who does thieve!
Ah, well you know
Yet won't declare him so!

MEPHISTOPHELES (*approaching the fire*).
And what is this pot?

MONKEYS. The innocent sot!
He don't know the pot,
Or even the kettle!

MEPHISTOPHELES. Be civil at least,
You ill-mannered beast!

MALE MONKEY. Take up the whisk, and sit on the settle!
(*He presses Mephistopheles to be seated.*)

FAUST (*who meanwhile has been standing before a mirror, sometimes drawing closer, sometimes stepping back from it*).

Now dare I trust my eyes? What heavenly sight
Is mirrored here in magic for my gaze?
O spirit of love, bear me in wingèd flight
To be her neighbour in her lovely ways.
Strange, that I lose her if my vision strays
From just this place: if nearer steps I dare,
I only see her through a sort of haze,
The picture of a woman passing fair.
And can a woman have such loveliness?
And from her living body, lying there,
Comes there indeed all heaven my soul to bless?
Has earth a gift so exquisite and rare?

MEPHISTOPHELES.

Of course: for when a god has toiled six days,
And says Bravo, and gives himself the praise,
The finished product should be debonair.
But take your time, gaze to your heart's content:
I'll find a beauty just as opulent,
And make her yours; and happy is his fate
Who teaches such a bride the married state.

(*Faust continues to gaze upon the mirror. Mephistopheles, sprawling on the settle, toys with the whisk, and goes on speaking.*)

Here like a thronèd king I sit me down,
With this my sceptre – but I lack a crown.

THE ANIMALS (*who meanwhile have been making sundry strange gestures, now bring Mephistopheles a crown, with shrill cries*).

Ah, pray be so good,
With sweat and with blood,
This head-dress to prime.

Witch's Kitchen 115

(*They carry the crown clumsily and break it into two pieces, with which they then jump about.*)
Now is it done!
We talk and look on,
And listen and rhyme –
FAUST (*looking towards the mirror*).
My reason swoons, with vision so sublime.
MEPHISTOPHELES (*looking towards the animals*).
My own top-storey starts to feel the worse.
ANIMALS. And if we have luck,
Then people are struck
With our serious verse.
FAUST (*indicating the glass*).
With fiery thoughts my heart begins to ache:
Let us go swiftly forth upon our way.
MEPHISTOPHELES (*indicating the animals*).
One thing at least emerges: no mistake,
These are the genuine poets of the day.
(*The cauldron, that the female monkey has meanwhile neglected, begins to boil over, and a great flame arises, that blazes up the chimney. The witch comes down through the flame with horrible cries.*)
THE WITCH. Ai-ow, ai-ow!
Damnable beast, accursèd sow!
Sending your kettle up in flame,
Cursèd beasts, to scorch your dame!
(*Perceiving Faust and Mephistopheles.*)
What's this to-do?
Who, pray, are you?
What are you seeking,
Prying and sneaking?
Blasted with groans,
Hell roast your bones!

(She smacks the ladle into the cauldron and spatters flames at Faust, Mephistopheles and the apes. The animals whimper.)

MEPHISTOPHELES *(reversing the whisk in his hand and hitting out among the glasses and pots).*

With a splash and a dash,
The glasses can crash,
And spilt is the hash!
A jovial mime,
My carrion loon!
For I beat the time,
While you sing the tune.

(The witch draws back in hate and fury.)

Old bag of bones, can you not recognize
Your lord and master, here before your eyes?
You scare-crow, what shall hold my sentence back,
That blots you out, you and your monkey-pack?
See you the scarlet jerkin, and not tremble?
Too blind the cockerel's feather to perceive?
When have you known my countenance dissemble?
Or must I wear my title on my sleeve?

THE WITCH. My Lord, forgive me, if I weren't genteel!
I missed the signs; I see no cloven heel,
And where, pray, be your jet-black raven-pair?

MEPHISTOPHELES.

Well, for this once, your lack of etiquette
Shall be excused; because, to be quite fair,
Much water's passed the bridges since we met.
Society's improved at every level,
And culture spreads now, even to the Devil.
Gone is the spook that filled the North with awe,
Out-moded are the horns, and tail and claw.
Touching the foot, with which I can't dispense,
My social circle might well take offence;

Witch's Kitchen

And so, like many fashionable lads,
I falsify my calves by using pads.

THE WITCH. Out of my wits I am, with the surprise,
To see Squire Satan here before my eyes.

MEPHISTOPHELES.
That name, good woman, you will please omit!

THE WITCH.
But why? That's nought to make a body quail.

MEPHISTOPHELES.
True, it is almost turned to fairy-tale,
And yet mankind has failed to benefit –
The Evil One is banned: evils prevail.
Call me Lord Marquis, then our trade is good;
I am a cavalier, like all the rest,
So cast no doubt upon my gentle blood,
Behold, my coat-of-arms – this for a crest!

(*He makes an indecent gesture.*)

THE WITCH (*laughing*).
Now that's the real old style of devil-may-care!
A rogue you are, a rogue you always were.

MEPHISTOPHELES (*to Faust*).
My friend, for your instruction I submit
The way to handle witches – this is it.

THE WITCH. But tell me, Sirs, the business you pursue.

MEPHISTOPHELES. A glassful of your celebrated brew,
The secret cordial – but well matured,
Its potency with strength of years ensured.

THE WITCH. Ay, gladly! Here's a bottle on my shelf,
From which I sometimes take a nip myself;
A juice, moreover, that has lost its stink,
A liquor I am very pleased to give.
(*Sotto voce.*) But if this man comes uninformed to drink,
You know full well, he's not an hour to live.

MEPHISTOPHELES.
> He is my friend, the brew will suit him well:
> I grant him all your kitchen can produce.
> Draw, then, your circle, speak your magic spell,
> And serve a bumper of the secret juice.
>> (*The Witch, with outlandish gestures, marks out a circle and places strange things in it. Meanwhile the glasses begin to ring and the cauldron to hum, making sounds of music. Lastly, she brings out a great book, and when she has arranged the monkeys in the circle, to serve her as a desk, and as torchbearers, she beckons Faust to draw near.*)

FAUST (*to Mephistopheles*).
> Nay, tell me, why this queer parade of antic,
> This gibbering witch-craft, running wild and frantic?
> For I have known and hated, long enough,
> The charlatanry of this senseless stuff.

MEPHISTOPHELES.
> That's slap-stick, man, for laughter and delight.
> Why be so sober-sided and sedate?
> This hocus-pocus is a doctor's right,
> To guarantee the dose will operate.
>> (*He prevails upon Faust to enter the circle.*)

THE WITCH (*with solemn emphasis begins to declaim from the book*).
> Now this understand:
> Make one into ten,
> Drop two out of hand,
> Three balance again,
> Then you are rich,
> On the word of the witch.
> From five and six
> The four transfix,
> Make seven and eight

Witch's Kitchen 119

    Fulfilling the fate:
    And nine makes one,
    And ten is none,
    And witches' one-times-one is done.
FAUST. The ravings of a crazy crone are these.
MEPHISTOPHELES.
    There's still a deal to follow, if you please.
    So runs the book: I recognize its style,
    I've read it much, a study worth the while,
    For if a work completely flouts the rules
    Its mystery enthralls both wise and fools.
    New art, my friend, springs from antiquity,
    And down the ages, civil or uncouth,
    Men practise three and one, and one and three,
    To substitute the error for the truth.
    And so they teach and babble undeterred
    – With fools there's not a hope of intervening –
    And when the people hear a sounding word
    They stand convinced that somewhere there's a meaning.
THE WITCH (*continuing*). The lofty might
    Of wisdom's light
    From all the world is hidden.
    The vacant mind
    Has truth assigned,
    It comes to him unbidden.
FAUST. How raves this ancient cabal-crier?
    Her nonsense makes my head go round!
    Stupidity's Gargantuan choir
    Is concentrated in the sound!
MEPHISTOPHELES.
    Redoubtable Sibyl, that will be enough:
    Give now the potion, and dispense the stuff
    With lavish hand, to over-brim the bowl.

My friend will drink no ruin from your craft,
For here we have a deeply learned soul,
That's tried the strength of many a potent draught.
   (*The Witch, with ceremony, pours the liquor into a goblet. As Faust lifts it to his lips, a pale flame arises from it.*)
MEPHISTOPHELES. Down with it, man, don't hesitate!
   'Twill send a glow of joy through all your frame.
   What, call yourself the devil's intimate,
   Yet flinch before the flicker of a flame!
   (*The Witch dissolves the circle. Faust steps out.*)
MEPHISTOPHELES. Up and away! You mustn't rest.
THE WITCH. And from the drink, Sir, may you benefit!
MEPHISTOPHELES (*to the Witch*).
   And if you have a favour to request,
   Upon Walpurgis Night just mention it.
THE WITCH. Now here's a ballad: sing it, and you'll find
   A marvellous effect is guaranteed.
MEPHISTOPHELES. Pay no heed, but follow my lead:
   A perspiration is your urgent need,
   To drive the ichor with a coursing speed
   Within, without, through body, heart and mind;
   And then I'll teach the use of lordly leisure,
   And soon will you perceive, with thrilling pleasure,
   How Cupid stirs your thoughts on womankind.
FAUST. Ah, let me to the mirror where I stood,
   To see that regal loveliness afresh.
MEPHISTOPHELES.
   Nay, nay, that paragon of womanhood
   Shall soon reward your gazing in the flesh.
   (*Aside.*) A dose like that within your guts, my boy,
   And every other wench is Helen of Troy.

A STREET

Faust, then Margareta passing by.

FAUST. Pray take my arm, fair lady. Let me dare
 To give you escort homeward, if I may.
MARGARETA. No ladyship am I, nor am I fair,
 And need no escort, Sir, to find my way. (*Exit.*)
FAUST. By Heaven, there goes a maid of rarest beauty:
 I never saw a girl more exquisite,
 With such an air of goodness and of duty,
 And yet the mettle of a lively wit.
 Her cheek's soft light, the crimson of her lips,
 Will shine for me, outlasting time's eclipse:
 For on my soul she printed, as she passed,
 Her looks so tender-eyed and so downcast;
 And in her brevity, when she replied,
 She seemed enchanting youth personified.
  (*Mephistopheles enters.*)
 Listen! The girl, go win her, Sir, for me!
MEPHISTOPHELES. The girl – what girl?
FAUST. That passed just now.
MEPHISTOPHELES. Oh, she?
 She's just been to her priest, in penitence
 Confessing sins; and he absolved the lot.
 I overheard her, lurking round the spot,
 And know her for a thing of innocence:
 Sinless the girl attends confession-hour,
 And over her the devil has no power.
FAUST. But, none the less, she must be turned fourteen.
MEPHISTOPHELES.
 There speaks the lad who plays the libertine,
 And thinks he has a right to every flower,

    Knowing no grace or honourable name
    Beyond his reach, to pluck it and devour;
    It often can't be done, Sir, all the same.
FAUST. Spare me, Professor Plausible, your saws
    And plaguey discourse on the moral laws.
    To cut the story short, I tell you plain,
    Unless her sweet young loveliness has lain
    Within my arms' embrace this very night,
    The stroke of twelve shall end our pact outright.
MEPHISTOPHELES.
    Consider the requirements of the case:
    A fortnight is the minimum of space,
    To engineer the proper time and place.
FAUST. Give me the girl and seven hours of grace:
    I wouldn't ask the devil for assistance,
    To overcome the little thing's resistance.
MEPHISTOPHELES.
    Quite like a rake of Paris, Sir, already!
    But I advise a strategy more steady,
    For what's the good of snatching at your joy?
    The pleasure's far more wonderful, my boy,
    If first you make a dainty to and fro,
    Prepare the darling with love's puppet-show,
    And pet her, like your novelistic stallions,
    After the manner of the best Italians.
FAUST. That's nothing to the hunger of my heart.
MEPHISTOPHELES.
    Pray hear me now, Sir, pleasantry apart,
    I tell you once for all, that lovely girl
    Is never to be taken in a whirl.
    We stand to lose by forcing of the pace,
    When gentle subterfuge would meet our case.
FAUST. Get me a trifle from that angel's nest,

Or lead me to the dwelling of my dove!
Get me the kerchief that has touched her breast,
Or bring her girdle for my thoughts of love!

MEPHISTOPHELES.
To prove to you the loyalty and zeal
With which I serve the passion that you feel,
I'll guide your eager steps without delay,
And you shall stand within her room this day.

FAUST. And shall I see her? – have her?

MEPHISTOPHELES. No, good Sir,
She's on a visit to a cottager;
But you, meanwhile, may pass sweet hours away
And breathe her aura to your heart's content,
And nurse the thoughts of love's enravishment.

FAUST. Can we go now?

MEPHISTOPHELES. It is too early yet.

FAUST.
Prepare a gift, the best that wealth can get. (*Exit.*)

MEPHISTOPHELES.
Presents, so soon? – He'll win her, past a doubt!
Full many a pretty place I know
With treasure buried long ago,
I'll go and get the baubles sorted out.

EVENING

A neat little room.

MARGARETA (*braiding and binding her hair*).
I would I knew who he may be
That stopped to-day and spoke to me.
He bore himself so gallantly
And with such grace,

I'm sure he is of noble race;
I read it in his brow and bearing –
Else had he never been so daring. (*Exit.*)
MEPHISTOPHELES. Step softly in, and be discreet.
FAUST (*after a moment's silence*).
Leave me alone: we'll later meet.
MEPHISTOPHELES (*prying around*).
Not every girl keeps things so neat. (*Exit.*)
FAUST. Now, welcome, twilight, weave your silken skein
Within this homely simple sanctuary,
And bring my heart the bitter-sweet of pain
That lives on dewy hope of love-to-be.
Here stillness breathes through every listening sense;
Here stays contentment, far from storm and stress,
And poverty enriched by innocence;
This little cell holds perfect happiness!
(*He throws himself upon the leather arm-chair beside the bed.*)
Receive my body, you whose friendly arms
Have generations borne, in joy or sadness,
Paternal throne of many fire-side charms,
Where children clustered in their loving gladness.
And she, perhaps, has curtseyed here and smiled
With joy to take her grandsire's Christmas gift,
And looked up, with the full cheeks of a child,
His faded hand to her young lips to lift.
Dear girl, your spirit steals upon my heart;
I feel your wealth, your order-loving mind,
That, like an angel of domestic art,
Sweetens your home with pride of womankind,
Lays the smooth cloth, strews on the floor the sand,
With such divinity within your gentle hand,
Your cottage holds a part of heaven enshrined.
And here! (*He draws one of the bed-curtains.*)

Evening

    I tremble in my joy, and sigh
With sweet desire to dream the hours away:
Here Nature wrought the stuff of dreams, whereby
There came an angel to the light of day.
    Here lay the child, through peaceful, innocent hours,
Her little bosom with the life-stream warmed,
And here, by weaving of mysterious powers,
Her countenance divine was softly formed.
    And you, good Sir: your purpose here, your quest?
How moved and troubled is my cloudy breast!
What make you here? Why is your heart so sore?
Ah, wretched Faust, I know you now no more!
    And what enchanted atmosphere is this?
I thought to follow hot on passion's flair,
And now I languish for a true-love's bliss:
Are we the sport of every breath of air?
    And came she now, this moment, in this place,
How would you sicken in your guilty flame?
The upstart lout, grown small, would hide his face,
And grovel at her feet, dissolved in shame.

MEPHISTOPHELES (*entering*).
    Come, quick! She's turned the corner of the lane!
FAUST. Away, for never, never will I come again!
MEPHISTOPHELES. Here is a casket, good and heavy,
    I got it by a private levy:
Quick, lay it in her coffer there,
Here's stuff to turn her head, I swear;
For though I put the trinkets in
Thinking another lass to win,
A girl's a girl, and fair is fair.
FAUST. Shall I, or not?
MEPHISTOPHELES.   Why stand and stare?
    Perhaps you plan to keep the treasure!

If so, please temper your caprice
And moderate your avarice,
Wasting my labour and my leisure!
I hope it's not by greed you're led:
I rack my brains and scratch my head –
(He quickly places the casket in the coffer, which he locks.)
Away, with speed! –
I study your desire and need,
To win for you a lovely girl,
And there you stand
As if you'd lecture-notes in hand,
A proper professorial churl,
So overwhelmed, one might suppose
Physics and metaphysics grey
Had come to life before your nose.
Away! *(Exeunt.)*

MARGARETA *(entering with a lamp)*.
How close it is, so sultry here!
        (She throws open the window.)
Yet out of doors 'tis not so warm.
I feel, 'tis strange, a sort of fear –
I wish my mother would come home.
I am a frightened silly thing,
To start this foolish shuddering.
        (She begins to undress, singing the while.)
  In Thule there reigned a monarch,
And he was true till death.
A golden cup his mistress
Gave him, with parting breath.

  That was his dearest chalice,
No other did he prize,
And ever, as he raised it,
The tears stood in his eyes.

Evening

   Then came his time of dying,
His wealth of state was told;
He left his heir his treasure,
Except his cup of gold.
   Surrounded by his vassals
A royal feast held he,
High in the castle's state-room,
Ancestral, by the sea.
   There stood the royal master,
Drank, in life's sunset glow,
And hurled the sacred goblet
To the ocean, deep below.
   He saw it plunge and founder
And sink deep in the sea.
The light sank from his vision,
And never again drank he.
   (*She opens the coffer, to put away her clothes, and sees the casket.*)
How comes this lovely casket in my box?
I well remember fastening the locks.
'Tis very strange. What can there be inside?
Perhaps it's left as some security
Against a loan my mother has supplied.
Here by a ribbon hangs a little key:
I'll open it, and solve the mystery.
Dear God!
What lovely things! More dazzling fair
Than any I could hope to see!
These jewels a marchioness could wear
In the most splendid company.
How would the necklace look on me?
Whose can they be,
These gems so brilliant and rare?

(She puts some of the jewels on, then goes to her mirror.)
These earrings, how I wish them mine!
They lend at once a different air.
For men may think it very fine
To call a poor girl young and fair;
It doesn't lead you anywhere –
Half-pitying is the praise we must endure.
The lure of gold
Has power to hold
The hearts of all: alas for all us poor.

A WALK

*Faust pacing to and fro, deep in thought.
Mephistopheles joins him.*

MEPHISTOPHELES.
 By love that's scorned, by all the fires of hell,
 And any curse
 That's worse
 Piled on as well!
FAUST.
 What ails you, man? And why this dire grimace?
 I never yet encountered such a face.
MEPHISTOPHELES. I'd have the devil take me instantly,
 Only it happens I myself am he.
FAUST. Is this a play, or have you lost your wits?
 The madman is a part your talent fits.
MEPHISTOPHELES.
 Those jewels, that Margareta should have got,
 A damned old parson's pocketed the lot!
 The things came to the notice of her mother,
 Which put her conscience in a secret pother:

A Walk

She has a flair for nosing troubles out,
Always in prayer-books is her sniffing snout;
She'll smell the furniture, to make it plain
Whether a thing be sacred or profane.
So at the jewellery she gives one sniff,
And diagnoses evil in the whiff.
'My child,' she cries, 'be sure ill-gotten wealth
Will snare the soul, and undermine the health.
To Blessed Mary shall the jewels be given,
And she will send us manna down from heaven.'
Poor Gretchen laughed the wrong side of her face.
She thought 'A gift horse' summarized the case;
Besides, she felt that such a handsome giver
Could not be godless or an evil-liver.
The mother fetched a priest without delay,
And he, no sooner was the story uttered,
Knew pretty well which side his bread was buttered.
Said he, 'My daughter, in the narrow way
That leads to life, you show a proper spirit;
For he that overcometh shall inherit.
The Church can swallow gold and lands and such,
And never feel that she has had too much;
For only to the Church there appertains
A good digestion for ill-gotten gains.'

FAUST. A saying true of others too:
A king, for instance, or a Jew.

MEPHISTOPHELES.
He sweeps the board of pendants, bracelets, rings,
Just like a woman with her shopping-things,
And coolly thanks them, ere he further struts,
As if they'd given him a dish of nuts;
Promised reward where heavenly joys abide,
And left them feeling highly edified.

FAUST. And Margareta?
MEPHISTOPHELES.   Sits in discontent,
  Unwilling to resign or to resent,
  Keeps dreaming of the casket's golden store
  And of the one who gave it, even more.
FAUST. It grieves me that my dearest love should fret.
  Go, get me jewels, a fresh and brilliant set:
  The first were nothing much to rave about.
MEPHISTOPHELES.
  Mere trifles, child's play to my lord, no doubt!
FAUST. Arrange the matter as I ask it:
  Visit her neighbour, see you're civil,
  Be not a wishy-washy devil,
  But look me out another casket.
MEPHISTOPHELES.
  My gracious lord, at your behest I fly! (*Exit Faust.*)
  Smitten like that, the fool will have his say,
  And puff the planets from the starry sky,
  To help his darling pass the time away.

NEIGHBOUR'S HOUSE

MARTHA (*alone*). Forgive my man, I say, good Lord,
  Him that went bolting off abroad,
  Content to treat me rough and raw,
  And leave me lonely on the straw.
  And yet, God knows, I never crossed him,
  But loved him well, and now I've lost him.
       (*She weeps.*)
  Ay me, perhaps he's breathed his parting breath –
  I wish I'd a certificate of death!
MARGARETA. Dame Martha!

Neighbour's House

MARTHA. Ay, what is it, girl?
MARGARETA. I faint with fear, I'm in a whirl.
  Another casket's come for me,
  Hid in my chest, of ebony,
  With things in it more lovely rare
  Than even in the first one were.
MARTHA. A girl were best not tell her mother,
  Or priests will have it, like the other.
MARGARETA. But look, just look at them, oh do!
MARTHA. You lucky little creature, you!
MARGARETA. I can't go out in them, alas,
  Either in town, or to the mass.
MARTHA. Come often over here to me,
  And dress up fine where none can see,
  And walk before the mirror here,
  A joy for both of us, my dear.
  Then comes a feast or holiday, maybe,
  When, piece by piece, you wear the jewellery –
  Pearls for your ears, a necklace: from your mother
  We'll hide them, or invent some tale or other.
MARGARETA.
  Whose is the hand that placed the caskets there?
  It seems somehow an ominous affair. (*A knock.*)
  Oh dear, my mother? – See who's at the door.
MARTHA (*peeping through the curtain*).
  A gentleman I've never seen before.
  Come in!
MEPHISTOPHELES. I thank you kindly, ma'am.
  I'm sorry to intrude, I am –
    (*He seems abashed at the presence of Margareta.*)
  With Martha Schwertlein I would speak.
MARTHA. That's me. What is it that you seek?
MEPHISTOPHELES. Enough for me that you are she:

You've high-born company, I see.
Excuse me for intruding, pray –
I'll look in later in the day.

MARTHA (*in a loud tone*).
Of all the things that I heard tell! –
He takes you for a demoiselle!

MARGARETA. I'm nothing but a poor young thing:
The gentleman is too flattering.
The jewels and trinkets aren't my own.

MEPHISTOPHELES. 'Tis not the jewellery alone;
She has an air, a glance so bright,
A man must count it a delight,
To be allowed to linger near.

MARTHA. But say what business brings you here.

MEPHISTOPHELES.
I wish I brought you news of better cheer,
I only hope I shan't be held to blame.
Your husband's dead: I greet you in his name.

MARTHA. Not dead! My own dear man! Alas the day!
My husband dead! Help, or I swoon away!

MARGARETA.
Dear neighbour, set your heart against despair!

MEPHISTOPHELES. And hear me tell the sorrowful affair.

MARGARETA. So may I never love, in fearful dread:
My heart would break, if that my love were dead.

MEPHISTOPHELES. No joy but has its sorrow – that is life.

MARTHA. Please tell me of the ending that he made.

MEPHISTOPHELES. We buried him in Padua, good wife,
His coffin at St. Anthony's is laid.
In consecrated ground and duly blest
He takes his cool and everlasting rest.

MARTHA.
And have you nothing more, no pledge to bring?

Neighbour's House

MEPHISTOPHELES.
  Ay, one request. His solemn bidding is
  Three hundred masses for his obsequies.
  And that is all – I've not another thing.
MARTHA. What! Not a lucky florin? Not a ring,
  Such as the workman saves beneath his kit,
  A keepsake he will guard where-e'er he wanders,
  And rather beg or starve than part with it!
MEPHISTOPHELES. Dear Madam, my regret is infinite,
  But, truly, he was not the sort that squanders.
  What sins he had afflicted him full sore,
  Ay, and his bad luck troubled him still more.
MARGARETA.
  Poor souls, alas, are saddened with such cares!
  And him I will remember in my prayers.
MEPHISTOPHELES.
  A charming girl like you, my pretty dear,
  Should surely think of getting wed.
MARGARETA. To wed? Nay, not for many a year!
MEPHISTOPHELES.
  No husband? Why then, take a lover instead:
  It is the sweetest gift of Heaven above,
  To fondle such a dear, and teach her love.
MARGARETA. Such ways are not our custom, Sir.
MEPHISTOPHELES. Custom or not, it does occur.
MARTHA. Please tell the rest –
MEPHISTOPHELES.   I watched him as he lay,
  In his last hour, upon a filthy bed –
  Not dung, but rotten straw. He passed away
  Quite as a Christian should, and grieved, he said,
  To have upon his conscience such a score.
  'How I must loathe my wretched self,' he cried,
  'Deserting wife and trade and chimney-side.

It's killing me, the wrong I do deplore:
If only she forgave me, ere I died!'
MARTHA (*weeping*).
Dear husband! I forgave him long before.
MEPHISTOPHELES.
'I was to blame,' he said, 'but she far more.'
MARTHA. Lies! At death's door!
To face the hour of death with such a lie!
MEPHISTOPHELES. If I know anything to judge him by,
He rambled as he neared the other shore.
'No chance had I for promenades,' he said;
'First I got children, then I got them bread;
When I say bread, the broadest sense is meant—
With mine I got no freedom or content.'
MARTHA. And this despite devotion on my part,
And all my drudgery by day and night!
MEPHISTOPHELES.
Not so, he had your memory at heart.
Said he, 'As Malta faded from my sight,
I prayed for wife and children fervently,
And Heaven answered me my prayer aright:
Our vessel chased a Turkish barque to sea,
And found she had the Sultan's gold on board.
Then gallantry came in for its reward,
And I for my part, as was only fair,
Received a pretty fortune for my share.'
MARTHA. What's that? Where is it? Buried? Hid away?
MEPHISTOPHELES.
To the four winds it is, so who can say?
A belle of Naples took a fancy to him,
When all unfriended he had strolled her way,
And acts of such devotion did she do him,
That he could trace it to his dying day.

Neighbour's House

MARTHA.
> The wretch! To rob his children and his wife!
> No misery could school his wicked head,
> Or turn him from his shameful ways of life.

MEPHISTOPHELES.
> How true; but that's precisely why he's dead.
> And, frankly, if I now were in your shoes
> I'd watch a year of widow's weeds go past,
> Then look around another mate to choose.

MARTHA. Ay me, 'twere hard to find one like my last,
> In all the world there's not another such.
> No woman had a sweeter fool than mine,
> Only he took to roaming overmuch,
> And foreign women and the foreign wine,
> That, and a passion for the cursèd dice.

MEPHISTOPHELES.
> Well, well, that might have turned out very nice,
> If he had winked at waywardness in you.
> An easy rule for both is my advice:
> Upon these terms, why, I myself would woo,
> Buy you a ring, and promise to be true.

MARTHA. Oh, Sir, I'm sure you only speak in jest!

MEPHISTOPHELES (*aside*). This is my cue,
> Retreat were best,
> And that before there's more inferred.
> She'd hold the very devil to his word.
> (*Softly to Margareta.*) My pretty dear, has not your heart been stirred?

MARGARETA. What mean you, Sir?

MEPHISTOPHELES (*aside*). You charming, innocent thing!
> Ladies, adieu!

MARGARETA. Good-bye!

MARTHA.   Stay, can you bring

> The evidence I want? have certified
> Where he is buried, when and how he died?
> I like to see things done with law and order,
> And read them in the Saturday Recorder.

MEPHISTOPHELES.
> Two witnesses are needed for your case;
> Then, madam, truth will show an honest face.
> And luckily I have a first-class friend:
> On your behalf in court he can attend.
> I trust I may present him.

MARTHA. Oh, please do!

MEPHISTOPHELES.
> And will the dear young lady be there, too?
> A gallant lad, he is, has travelled wide,
> And knows how ladies should be gratified.

MARGARETA.
> Sir, I should blush, with looks fixed on the ground.

MEPHISTOPHELES.
> You have no need, though he were monarch crowned.

MARTHA. To-night, within my little garden, then,
> Behind the house, we'll wait the gentlemen.

A STREET

Faust and Mephistopheles meet.

FAUST. How now? What news? What chances of success?

MEPHISTOPHELES. Bravo, I like to see a lover keen.
> The girl is yours within a week, or less.
> To-night at neighbour Martha's she'll be seen:
> That woman seems to me expressly made
> To play the pimp or ply a gipsy's trade.

FAUST. Well done!

MEPHISTOPHELES. But something's asked of me and you.
FAUST. One turn deserves another as its due.
MEPHISTOPHELES.
  We only have to prove beyond a doubt
  Her lord and master lately was laid out
  In Padua, in consecrated soil.
FAUST. How wise of you! So now we make the journey?
MEPHISTOPHELES.
  Sancta simplicitas! – A needless toil:
  We swear an oath, and all the rest is blarney!
FAUST. If that's the best that you can do,
  Your precious plan has fallen through.
MEPHISTOPHELES.
  O man of virtue! Turning a new leaf!
  Is this the first affair in your career
  In which you gave false evidence? In brief,
  Have you not played the learned chanticleer
  Concerning God and universal themes
  And man and all his inmost thoughts and dreams?
  Prating with definitions all aglow,
  Grandiloquent of words and bold of breast?
  And now look close: if truth must be confessed,
  You understood as much as now you know
  Of Mr Schwertlein's final place of rest.
FAUST. Still the old liar of the Sophist school!
MEPHISTOPHELES.
  I wonder! – Try to keep your judgment cool;
  For will you not to-morrow do your best
  In honour's name poor Gretchen to befool,
  And the deep soul of love to her attest?
FAUST. And from the bottom of my heart.
MEPHISTOPHELES.   Dear me.
  No doubt you'll swear love's deathless constancy,

    Along with love's unique compelling urge:
    'Tis strange, what wonders from the heart emerge.
FAUST. No more! This holds! – If in my mind
    The turmoil lives, the flood and flame,
    So that I seek but never find
    Its most mysterious name;
    When heart and soul I range the earth
    To find a lofty word of worth,
    And still the same
    Answer return –
    I burn, I burn
    Eternally:
    Is this then empty sophistry
    And just a devil's game?
MEPHISTOPHELES. How right I was.
FAUST.   Now mark this, pray,
    And spare my strength of voice and lung:
    The speaker with one tune upon his tongue
    Will win the day.
    So come, I view this chatter with disgust,
    And bow to you, simply because I must.

IN MARTHA'S GARDEN

Faust. Margareta.

MARGARETA. I feel you're only condescending, Sir,
    Shaming the ignorance you wish to spare;
    For custom trains the courteous traveller
    To give to passing things a pleasant air.
    My homely talk can hold but little sense
    For one who has so much experience.
FAUST. One word, one glance of yours is worth

In Martha's Garden

More than the cleverness of all the earth. (*He kisses her hand.*)

MARGARETA.
Oh, Sir, not that! How can you kiss my hand?
It is so ugly and so rough!
So much I have to scour and scrub and sand,
Since for my mother I can never do enough.

Martha. Mephistopheles.

MARTHA. Your travels, Sir, can never cease, you say?

MEPHISTOPHELES.
Ah, business drives us to it, and our duty:
'Tis sad to stay in towns of restful beauty,
Knowing full well that we must break away.

MARTHA.
That sort of thing may work when one is young:
Careering round the world seems then so brave.
But luck will change, and bad times come along,
And then to creep alone towards one's grave,
A stiff old bachelor, is surely wrong.

MEPHISTOPHELES. I shudder when I think of such a fate.

MARTHA. Then, Sir, take heed before it is too late.

Faust. Margareta.

MARGARETA. So easy are you with your courtesy,
And out of sight, they say, is out of mind;
And then so many friends, Sir, you can find,
Far cleverer than me.

FAUST. Dear girl, believe me, so-called cleverness
Is often vanity and mere pretence.

MARGARETA. How so?

FAUST. I mean that true souls hardly guess
The sacred worth of their own innocence;
Yet simple love and meekness are sublime,
The sweetest gifts of Nature's bounteous grace –

MARGARETA. Ah, think of me one little moment's space:
  To think of you, I shall have ample time.
FAUST. Are you then much alone?
MARGARETA. Well, yes. I own
  Our household is a little one,
  But still, there's plenty to be done.
  We have no maid: the need to cook, and clean,
  And sew, and cater, keeps me on the run.
  In all the details of routine,
  My mother is a paragon,
  In fact,
  She's terribly exact.
  Not that she needs to cut expenses down:
  We can afford a better style than many.
  My father left for us a pretty penny,
  With house and garden, just outside the town.
  Yet nowadays a quiet life I pass:
  My brother is a soldier, now abroad;
  My little sister – she is dead, alas.
  With her I had my share of toil and pain,
  But gladly would I do the same again:
  She was a child that I adored.
FAUST. She was an angel, if she was like you.
MARGARETA.
  I brought her up; she loved me dearly, too.
  After my father's death, the child was born;
  Hope for my mother hovered in despair,
  So ill she lay, so wretched and forlorn.
  Slowly her strength returned with months of care,
  But being frail, from fever so severe,
  No thought there was that she could feed the mite,
  And so I had the little thing to rear,
  With milk and water, watching day and night.

In Martha's Garden

    Content upon my lap it seemed my own,
    And in my arms it nestled with delight,
    And soon, with busy limbs, was sweetly grown.
FAUST. The purest human happiness was yours.
MARGARETA.
    And yet I went through many anxious hours:
    By night its little cradle I would keep
    Close to my bed, and if it stirred or cried
    I woke from sleep
    To give it food, or take it to my side;
    Or, if it fretted still, I had to rise
    And dandle it about,
    And pace the little room to hush its cries.
    Yet, early in the morning, I was out
    Tending the washing-trough with heavy eyes.
    Then there were chores or marketing to do,
    And so the same old thing the whole year through.
    With such a moil,
    One's spirits are not always of the best;
    And yet our toil
    Makes food taste sweeter, so that we are bless'd,
    And grateful for our rest.
            Martha. Mephistopheles.
MARTHA. Ah, we poor women have a fine to-do
    To lead you bachelors the proper way.
MEPHISTOPHELES.
    Then surely it's for someone such as you
    To show me kindly where I go astray.
MARTHA. But, Sir, have you not known a tender flame,
    Or someone very special in your life?
MEPHISTOPHELES.
    The proverb tells us, love of home and wife
    Is wealth past price of gold or pearls or fame.

MARTHA. But have you no desire towards womankind?
MEPHISTOPHELES.
  Folk make themselves agreeable, I find.
MARTHA. I mean to say, Sir, have you never learned
  The seriousness with which the heart can ache?
MEPHISTOPHELES. I've learned that it is always a mistake
  To speak in jest where ladies are concerned.
MARTHA. Oh, you mistake me!
MEPHISTOPHELES.   My apologies!
  At least I don't mistake your courtesies.

Faust. Margareta.

FAUST. And so you knew that we had met before,
  And at your gate, my dove, you recognized me.
MARGARETA.
  You knew that, from my eyes and lowered look.
FAUST. Will you forgive the liberty I took?
  My own audacity surprised me,
  So to accost you by the minster-door.
MARGARETA. I blushed indeed, for this was new to me.
  None could speak ill of me; and yet such daring
  Must prove, I thought, some looseness in my bearing:
  Oh dear, thought I, some boldness he can see
  From which at once he's taken it for granted,
  So light a girl would give him all he wanted.
  Yet, feeling in me stirred, I can't deny,
  Pleading your cause – I know not how it grew –
  And very angry with myself was I,
  Because I wasn't angrier with you.
FAUST. You darling!
MARGARETA.   Wait! (*She picks a marguerite and plucks the petals.*)
FAUST.   What then? – A daisy-chain?
MARGARETA. Only a game.

In Martha's Garden

FAUST. How so?
MARGARETA. You'll think it vain,
And laugh at me. (*She murmurs as she plucks the flower.*)
FAUST. What are you murmuring?
MARGARETA. He loves me – loves me not.
FAUST. Dear, heavenly thing!
MARGARETA. He loves me – not, he loves me – not,
He loves me!
FAUST. Ay, sweet child, the heavenly powers
Are talking to you with the tongue of flowers:
So let it be. He loves you. Deep, ah deep,
The meaning seeks an answer in your heart.
MARGARETA. Ah, how I tremble.
FAUST. No sighs or trembling! Look in my eyes,
And let them, let this handclasp say to you
Things beyond human speech.
Ah love, wholly to yield one's self, to know
Deep bliss that has no ending!
Marked for eternity, so deep,
This cannot end – unless despair were all!
Nay, there's no ending then.
(*Margareta clasps his hand, then frees herself and runs from him. For a moment he ponders, then he follows her.*)
MARTHA (*entering*). The night is falling.
MEPHISTOPHELES. Ay, and we must go.
MARTHA. I would have asked you gladly, Sir, to stay,
But in this wicked place they gossip so.
You'd think they'd naught to do the livelong day
But watch their neighbours passing to and fro,
And peek and pry, and so the rumours grow:
One acts with care,
But still they have their say.
Where's the young pair?

MEPHISTOPHELES.　　　　　They lightly flit and stray
　Like butterflies.
MARTHA.　　　　　He seems her way inclined.
MEPHISTOPHELES. And she no less for him, you'll find:
　That is the world's old way.

A SUMMER-HOUSE

Margareta runs in, slips behind the door and, with fingers lightly on her lips, looks out through the crevice.

MARGARETA. He's coming.
FAUST.　　　　　Minx, so now you're teasing me!
　I have you now. (*He kisses her.*)
MARGARETA (*returning his kiss*).
　Oh, dearest man, I love you from my heart.
FAUST. Who's there?
MEPHISTOPHELES.　A friend.
FAUST.　　　　　A brute!
MEPHISTOPHELES.　　　　　It's time for you to part.
MARTHA (*entering*). Ay, Sir, 'tis late.
FAUST.　　　　　May I not come your way?
MARGARETA. My mother, she – good-bye!
FAUST.　　　　　I leave you then?
　Good-bye.
MARTHA.　Adieu, and don't delay.
MARGARETA. Soon to return, ah soon to meet again!
　　　　(*Exeunt Faust and Mephistopheles.*)
　Heavens, what such a man can find
　To ponder over in his mind!
　And there I stand, a tongue-tied miss,
　And can no answer make but 'yes'.
　I cannot think what he can see
　In a poor ignorant girl like me.

FOREST AND CAVERN

FAUST (*alone*). All things are come to me, O mighty spirit!
All that I asked you gave me. Not in vain
You turned your visage towards me in the fire,
Bestowing Nature's splendour to be mine,
Ay, and with strength to hold her and enjoy.
Mine was no baffling of a cold encounter:
You taught me in her deepest heart to gaze,
To seek as in the bosom of a friend,
Beholding thus the train of living things,
And learning to perceive my very brothers
In sky and stream and in the silent glade.
Or, if the bounding tempest tears the forest
And giant pines come crashing on the crown
Of neighbour tree-tops, grinding branch and bole,
So that the mountain shakes with thud and shock,
You lead my steps within the sheltering cavern
Where I may meet my soul, and all the heart
Of wonder in my spirit stands revealed.
Now on my wakened soul the gentle moon
Arises pure and peaceful. Now there float,
From gleaming cliff and drenching dewy brake,
Pale shadowed phantoms from forgotten worlds
To silver the austerities of thought.

Now do I see, no perfect thing is given
To poor mankind. The bliss you have bestowed
To bear me ever nearer to the gods
Binds this companion to me: doomed I am
To need the help of him whose impudence
Ensures the cheap abasement of myself
In my own sight, so much his subtle word
Can sour and stifle all your gift of joy.

Thus burns within my breast the fire he kindles,
So that I hunger for that beauteous form,
Blundering with desire towards fruition,
And in fruition pining for desire.

MEPHISTOPHELES (*entering*).
What need, dear Sir, this dull life to pursue?
One loses pleasure in the same old view.
It's good no doubt
To try things out;
Then off we go to something really new.

FAUST. I would you had some better thing to do
Than plaguing me in my short hour of ease.

MEPHISTOPHELES. Well, take your rest. I'll say adieu,
The chance in fact I gladly seize:
A mad ungracious churl like you
Is mighty difficult to please.
A pretty handful, I must say!
One never knows, toil as one may,
What pleases him: no sign of grace
Is seen upon his lordship's face.

FAUST.
Ay, that's the style: first with his devil's pranks
He pesters me, and then awaits my thanks.

MEPHISTOPHELES.
And how, poor son of earth, would you
Have tried to live without my aid?
How do you think the cure was made
Of all the feverish to-do
That held your fantasy in thrall?
Without me, Sir, I'm much afraid
You'd have stepped off this earthly ball.
And now you'll haunt the caves alone
And choose a broody owl's abode,

>   Or sit on moss and clammy stone
>   And suck your nurture like a toad.
>   Sweet pastimes of an anchoret!
>   The Doctor's in your carcase yet.
> FAUST. You cannot know the fresh and living springs
>   From Nature's solitary places welling;
>   And, could you guess the solace that she brings,
>   Your devilry were quick to work its quelling.
> MEPHISTOPHELES. O noble, supernatural delight!
>   In dark and dewfall on the hills to lie,
>   And clasp the welkin to you in the night,
>   And swell in ecstasy divinely high,
>   To probe earth's secret core in agitation
>   And hug to heart the six days of creation,
>   To feel the Lord knows what of joy and pride,
>   And reach love's all-pervading blissful tide:
>   Your Son of Earth, transcending his condition,
>   Then brings his noble new-born intuition –
>   (*He makes an unseemly gesture.*)
>   I hardly like to say to what fruition.
> FAUST. Shame on you, man!
> MEPHISTOPHELES.   Ah, now you're put about,
>   And claim the moral right to cry 'For shame',
>   Because chaste ears must never hear the name
>   Of things chaste hearts will never go without.
>   But patience, friend, and let us still be lenient:
>   Lie to yourself whenever it's convenient.
>   But not for long one stands the pace.
>   You show already wear and tear;
>   If it goes on, black doubt and care,
>   And madness too, will leave their trace.
>   Enough of this! Your little love sits there
>   Disconsolate. No solace can she find.

She cannot put your image from her mind,
And all because she loves you to despair.
First came your wave of passion past control,
As when the snow melts, and the stream runs high;
This torrent you let loose upon her soul,
But now, it seems, the river's running dry.
May I suggest our mighty man thinks good
To leave majestic posing in a wood
And, stepping from his citadel above,
Rewards the poor young monkey for her love.
For her the time drags on a weary pace.
Her little face
Haunts by her window. On my word,
I saw her there, just gazing at the sky,
And never once she stirred.
An old refrain,
'Were I a bird'
Comes, as she sees the clouds drift by
Over the city wall, to mock her pain.
Except for that, her only song is sighing;
And often it is plain
She has been crying.
And then the wretched girl will try
To smile again,
Though loving fit to die.

FAUST. You snake of snakes!

MEPHISTOPHELES (*aside*). Agreed – if the poison takes.

FAUST. Damnable villain, go your cursèd ways,
Nor dare to speak that lovely creature's name.
Tempt not again my aching soul to gaze
On her sweet limbs with all my heart aflame.

MEPHISTOPHELES.
What's then to do? She thinks you've run away,

Forest and Cavern

    Which, more or less, is true, I'm bound to say.
FAUST. Nay, I am near her still: at home, abroad,
    I lose her not. My love is infinite.
    I'm jealous of the Body of the Lord
    When with her tender lips she touches it.
MEPHISTOPHELES.
    Well said, my friend! I've envied you indeed
    Those twin delights that in the roses feed.
FAUST. Pander, be gone!
MEPHISTOPHELES.   Ay, scold! And I will laugh.
    The god who fashioned boy and girl will tell
    He never did the noble job by half,
    But found them opportunity as well.
    Why do you moan and ring your true-love's knell?
    You should be making for your sweetheart's room,
    Not looking for a tomb.
FAUST. What means that ecstasy upon her breast?
    What though her bosom lulls my heart to rest –
    Do I not know myself to be her doom?
    I, the uprooted, I the homeless jade,
    The monster I, whose only aim is this:
    To scour the rocks like any blind cascade
    Racing and eager for the dark abyss.
    While she from passion sweetly lived aloof,
    With senses of a scarcely wakened child,
    The alpine paddock and the cottage roof
    Her busy tender world and undefiled.
    And I, the curse of God upon my brow,
    I, not content
    To grip the rocks and make them bow
    And leave them rent,
    Must undermine her innocence as well,
    And make of her a sacrifice for Hell.

Help, Devil, to cut short the agony.
Whatever is to come, let quickly come.
Now may her fate come crashing down on me,
And drag her with me to the self-same doom!

MEPHISTOPHELES.
Ay, now it works again, and seethes and glows!
Go in, you precious fool, and comfort her!
Be not of those
Who think the doomsday is at hand, dear Sir,
Unless they see their path before their nose.
Long live the lad who follows up his bent –
And you have quite a gift for devilment.
No object is in viler taste, I'll swear,
Than a poor devil stricken with despair.

MARGARETA'S ROOM

She is alone at her spinning wheel.

My peace is gone,
My heart is sore,
It is gone for ever
And evermore.

Life without him
Is mere distress:
My eyes grow dim
With bitterness.

No way to reason
Can I find:
Wild fancies flutter
Over my mind.

My peace is gone,
My heart is sore,

It is gone for ever
And evermore.
  For him alone
I watch all day,
Only for him
From home I stray.
  His stride and style,
So noble and wise,
His lips when they smile,
And the shine of his eyes!
  The sound of his words
Is honey and bliss,
The touch of his hand,
And oh, his kiss!
  My peace is gone,
My heart is sore,
It is gone for ever
And evermore.
  My bosom stirs,
My heart will pine
To touch him and hold him
And have him for mine,
  And kiss him too
My joy to crown,
And let his kisses
My senses drown.

MARTHA'S GARDEN

Margareta. Faust.

MARGARETA. Promise me, Heinrich!
FAUST.   Dear, I promise true.

MARGARETA. Please tell me what religion means to you.
　Although I think you very good and kind,
　I doubt if worship weighs much in your mind.
FAUST. Let be, dear child! You feel my love is sure:
　For those I love, death's pangs I would endure,
　Nor any man of church or faith bereave.
MARGARETA. But that's not right: we must believe.
FAUST. We must?
MARGARETA. 　　　Why yes – forgive that I persist:
　You don't regard the Holy Eucharist.
FAUST. Regard it, yes.
MARGARETA. 　　　　But not with faith or need:
　You never go to mass, or say your creed.
　Do you believe in God?
FAUST. 　　　　　　　　Sweet, who can dare
　To say that he believes?
　Ask anywhere –
　A sage or priest – and you will see
　The answer seems like mockery
　Upon the asking.
MARGARETA. 　　　Then you don't believe?
FAUST. Nay, darling girl, no need to misconceive.
　For who can say that name
　And claim
　A very certain faith?
　Or where is he with feeling
　Of some revealing
　Who dares to say it is a wraith?
　He that's upholding
　All and enfolding,
　Holds he not,
　Folds he not
　You, me, himself?

Martha's Garden

    Towers not the vault of heaven above us?
Does not earth's fabric bear us bravely up?
Do not the friendly eyes of timeless stars
Still gleam upon our sight?
Gaze we for nought in one another's eyes?
Is not life teeming
Around the head and heart of you,
Weaving eternal mysteries
Seen and unseen, even at your side?
Oh, let them fill your heart, your generous heart,
And, when you lose your being in that bliss,
Give it what name you will –
Your joy, love, heart, your God.
For me, I have no name
To give it: feeling's surely all.
Names are but noise and smoke,
Obscuring heavenly light.

MARGARETA. All that is very good and right:
    Our pastor nearly says the same,
    Only his words are somewhat different.

FAUST. Beneath the sun
    From many hearts the self-same cry is sent:
    Each has his way and speech. Then will you blame
    My offering as irreverent?

MARGARETA.   What now I hear
    Were well enough, if I were reconciled;
    But something fails, and terribly I fear
    You have not Christ within.

FAUST.   My child!

MARGARETA. Alas, alas, it troubles me
    To see you in such company.

FAUST. How so?

MARGARETA.   The person who accompanies you

    Fills me with horror through and through.
    Nothing has chilled me since my life began,
    As does the dreadful visage of this man.
FAUST. My gentle darling, have no fear.
MARGARETA.
    Nay, but my blood runs cold when he is near.
    I'm fond of people, wish them well,
    I long to see you more than I can tell,
    But sight of him is like an evil spell.
    What's more, I take him for a cheat:
    If I am wrong, God's pardon I entreat.
FAUST. To make a world, strange fellows there must be.
MARGARETA. I wouldn't live in that man's company.
    There at my door, as soon as he steps in,
    He looks around him with a mocking grin
    And bitter wrath.
    One sees he cares for nothing: it stands forth
    Writ on his forehead, clear as on a scroll,
    That he can never love a living soul.
    I feel so happy on your arm,
    Surrendering, yielding, loving, warm,
    And then his presence shrivels up my heart.
FAUST. Dear love, how easily you take alarm.
MARGARETA. This strikes me like a fatal dart,
    That when he comes, or is a looker-on,
    I even feel my love for you is gone.
    Besides, when he is near I cannot pray,
    That is a fear that eats my heart away.
    And, Heinrich,'tis the same with you, I know.
FAUST. This is a mere aversion.
MARGARETA.   I must go.
FAUST. Grant me one hour on love's most sacred shores
    To clasp the bosom that my soul adores,

Martha's Garden

    Lie heart to heart and merge my soul in yours.
MARGARETA. Ah, if I only slept alone,
    You should find open doors
    This very night!
    But mother sleeps so light,
    And if our secret love were known
    That hour would surely be my last.
FAUST. Then, angel, all our cares are past.
    Here is a phial. In her cup
    Three little drops you have to shake,
    And softest dreams will seal her slumber up.
MARGARETA.
    What will I not perform for your sweet sake?
    But she, I trust, will take no harm from this.
FAUST. Dear girl, I would not counsel you amiss.
MARGARETA.
    Oh, dearest Heinrich, at your look, your touch,
    Comes something strange to over-ride my will,
    For you, already, I have done so much,
    That, in a way, there's nothing to fulfil. (*Exit.*)
MEPHISTOPHELES (*entering*).
    Your monkey, has she gone?
FAUST.   Still do you spy?
MEPHISTOPHELES.
    Why yes, I heard the lot in passing by,
    And stood apprized
    Of how our learned man was catechized;
    I hope, Sir Doctor, that you passed the test.
    Girls always have a lively interest
    To see the good old creed is not despised:
    If there he bends his manly neck, think they,
    He certainly will honour and obey.
FAUST. You monster, have you then no eyes

    To see this true and loving soul
    Grieved that her faith,
    To her the whole
    Assurance of the spirit's living breath,
    Fails in her lover, mid the shoal
    Of doubts in which she sees him borne to death?

MEPHISTOPHELES. Dear supersensual sensualist, a flirt,
    A little damsel, leads you by the nose.

FAUST. Abortive spawn of fire and dirt!

MEPHISTOPHELES.
    And what a gift in physiognomy she shows!
    My presence fills her with – she knows not what.
    She scents a djinn, no end of a bad lot,
    And in my gib she traces secret force,
    Perhaps the very Devil's intercourse.
    And now, to-night –?

FAUST.   What's that to you?

MEPHISTOPHELES. I have my bit of pleasure in it too.

AT THE WELL

Margareta and Lisbeth with pitchers.

LISBETH. Nothing of Barbara have you heard?

MARGARETA. Nay, not a word.
    You know I go out rarely.

LISBETH. She's played the little fool, that bird,
    And, Sibyl tells me, fallen fairly.
    There's breeding for you!

MARGARETA.   Why?

LISBETH.   A nice to-do!
    For when she eats and drinks she's feeding two.

MARGARETA. Ah!

At the Well

LISBETH. Well, in the end, it serves her right;
    For months she's hardly let him from her sight.
    What with her high-born canting,
    Her promenades and gallivanting,
    Always she had to be the first,
    At fairs or dances she must shine,
    Courted with cakes and treated to wine,
    Accepting his presents, void of honour,
    Not shamed to take so much upon her.
    And then all the billing and cooing they had;
    And our little blossom has gone to the bad.
MARGARETA. The poor young thing.
LISBETH. Is that all you say!
    When the likes of us were at spinning all day,
    Our mothers keeping us strictly at night,
    While she and lover could take their delight
    On the bench, in the porch, or up the dark walk;
    Nothing was counted too long for their talk.
    So let her repent, now the story's complete,
    And stand in the church in a sinner's white sheet.
MARGARETA. But surely he will take her as his wife.
LISBETH. And play the simple fool? Not on your life!
    He's other loves, a dashing lad.
    Besides, he's gone.
MARGARETA. But that is really bad.
LISBETH. If she should get him, we will make her sad:
    The boys will snatch the garland from her head,
    And we will strew her door with chaff instead. (*Exit.*)
MARGARETA (*alone*). What sounding things I used to say
    When some poor girl had gone astray!
    The sins of others to rebuff
    My tongue had never words enough.
    Black as it seemed, I'd blacken it,

No words seemed black enough to fit.
I blessed my stars, with airs so fine:
Now the reproach and sin are mine.
Yet all that urged me so to do,
Dear God, it was so sweet and true.

A SHRINE IN THE RAMPARTS

*In a niche an image of the Mater Dolorosa,
with jugs of flowers.*

MARGARETA. Ah, look down,
  Thou rich in sorrow's crown,
  With the grace
  Of thy dear face,
  Upon the woe in which I drown.
    With piercèd heart
  And cruel smart
  Thou seest the death of Him, Thine own.
  Thy looks and sighs
  For Him and Thee arise
  To reach the Father's throne.
    Who can know
  The pangs of woe
  That leave their ache in every bone?
  The prayers I made,
  Trembling, afraid,
  Sweet Saint, are known
  To Thee alone.
    And wheresoe'er I turn
  Sorrow will burn and burn
  And anguish in my bosom start.
  Alone then with my fears,

Come tears on tears,
Come fit to break my heart.
   The flower-pots at my window,
Wet with my tears were they,
Where I had stooped to pick you
These flowers at break of day.
   And early came the sunlight,
Gold in my room it shed,
But I sat lost in sorrow,
In misery, on my bed.
   Save me, oh save, from death's distress,
From all this shame and bitterness!
Look down,
Thou rich in sorrow's crown,
In mercy heed
My pitiable need.

NIGHT

In the street by Gretchen's door.

VALENTINE. I have been merry in many a crowd
   Of lively comrades boasting loud,
   Each drinking to his favourite lass
   To pledge her honour with a glass.
   Then on my elbows I would lean,
   In quiet confidence serene,
   And listen while they bragged and cheered,
   Then smile and gently stroke my beard,
   And say, with brimming glass in hand,
   'Each to his taste; but in this land
   Where is a maiden to be found
   So truly fair and sweet and sound

As my dear Gretel? Tell me who
Is fit to tie my sister's shoe.'
'Hear, hear!' The glasses clinked around,
While many cried 'His words are true',
And 'pride of all her sex' said some,
So that the boasters all were dumb.
And now – a man could tear his hair
Or dash his brains out in despair! –
With innuendo's mocking glee
Each petty scoundrel sneers at me.
While, like a poor defaulter, I
At random words sit sweating hot,
And though I long to smash the lot
I cannot give to one the lie.

    Who's this, comes sneaking in the night?
– A couple, if I judge aright.
If it is he, why then, let drive!
He goes not from this place alive.

Faust. Mephistopheles.

FAUST. How flickers from yon window in the night
  The altar lamp with wavering watchful flame,
  And, even as that sacristy's dim light
  Shows timid in the gloom, I feel the same
  Thick clinging darkness gather on my soul.

MEPHISTOPHELES.
  And I feel like a tom-cat on the stroll,
  When sick with love he climbs the fire-escape,
  And over walls then streaks his shadowy shape.
  I exercise a sort of moral right
  In bits of thieving or of love's delight.
  Then through my members, Sir, will thrill and leap
  The love of our superb Walpurgis Night,
  When, two days hence, the vigil that we keep

Night

   Will more than compensate our loss of sleep!
FAUST. But surely soon the treasure will be seen:
   Are we not followed by its glimmering sheen?
MEPHISTOPHELES. The joy shall soon be yours, to lift
   The casket with the wondrous gift:
   'Twas filled, when last I had a squint,
   With golden sovereigns from the mint.
FAUST. Is there no jewel, then, or ring
   Fit to enhance my true-love's grace?
MEPHISTOPHELES. I think I noticed some such thing –
   A string of pearls would meet the case.
FAUST. Ay, good, for I am loath to go
   Without a present to bestow.
MEPHISTOPHELES. Sometimes a gentleman at large
   May take his pleasure free of charge;
   And, while the glittering stars in heaven throng,
   I'll treat you to a first-class work of art:
   In fact I'll sing a highly moral song
   The better to befool her silly heart.
   (*Sings.*) Sweet Katie, say
   What make you, pray,
   At break of day
   Outside your lover's door?
   He'll take, I swear,
   A maiden there,
   But forth she'll fare
   A maid, alas, no more.
     Judge it aright!
   'Tis ended quite,
   And so good-night,
   You poor unhappy thing.
   When love is warm,
   Trust no thief's arm:

    Reserve your charm
    Until you have the ring!
VALENTINE. By God, whose virtue will you mar,
    Ratcatcher, blast you, fresh from hell?
    The devil take your damned guitar
    And then the troubadour as well.
MEPHISTOPHELES. How sad! The lute is now a total loss.
VALENTINE. I promise next to break your head across.
MEPHISTOPHELES. Be bold, Sir Doctor, don't give way,
    Stick close to me, you can't miscarry.
    Out with your toasting-iron I say,
    You do the thrusting while I parry.
VALENTINE. Then parry that!
MEPHISTOPHELES.   Why not?
VALENTINE.   And that!
MEPHISTOPHELES.   Quite right.
VALENTINE. I think the very devil's in the fight!
    Hey, what comes over me? My arm is lame.
MEPHISTOPHELES. Thrust home!
VALENTINE.   Ah, God!
MEPHISTOPHELES.   Now is the puppy tame.
    Come, quick,
    Good Sir, we'll do the vanishing trick!
    There soon will be a murderous hullabaloo.
    Though with police I know just what to do,
    Assize invokes a name at which I stick.
MARTHA (*above*). Neighbours, come quick!
MARGARETA (*at the window*). Oh, bring a light!
MARTHA. There's been some brawling and a fight.
VOICE (*from the gathering people*).
    There's one upon the ground, as good as dead.
MARTHA (*coming out*).
    The murderers, which way have they fled?

Night

MARGARETA. But who lies here?
VOICE. It is your mother's son.
MARGARETA. Dear God almighty, no!
VALENTINE. I'm dying: that is easy said,
  And still more easy done.
  Stand not around with looks of dread,
  Nor moan, you women, but come near,
  My dying words to hear.
        (*They gather round him.*)
  My Gretel, you so young and sweet
  Should be more clever and discreet,
  Not blunder like a silly chit.
  And confidentially, what's more,
  I tell you that you are a whore,
  So make a job of it!
MARGARETA.
  Brother! Dear God! To give me such a name!
VALENTINE.
  The Lord God can be left out, in this game.
  The thing is done and, sad to say,
  It now must fare as best it may.
  You've started secretly with one,
  But others soon will scent the fun;
  You intrigue with a dozen men,
  And all the town can have you then.
    A new-born shame at first appears
  Secure in clandestine delight,
  And then, with muffled eyes and ears,
  She hides herself in veils of night.
  Then, when you would the creature slay,
  She grows up rank and waxes bold
  And shows herself by light of day,
  Though none the prettier to behold.

    The uglier her features grow,
    The more she puts herself on show.
      I speak as one who now foresees
    That honest citizens one day,
    As from a carcase of disease,
    From you, you whore, will shrink away.
    Then shall the heart within you falter,
    To look in eyes that sadly stare.
    For you, no golden chains to wear,
    Nor shall you then draw near the altar.
    No more, with collars of fine lace,
    At dances shall you take your ease,
    But hide yourself in some foul place
    With beggars, cripples and disease.
    Forgiveness be as God shall please,
    But here may you be blasted with disgrace.
MARTHA. Ask for your soul the Lord's redeeming,
    Not spend your parting breath blaspheming.
VALENTINE. Could I but reach your shrivelled shape,
    You pimping female jackanape,
    For all my sins I'd hope to find
    A grace entirely to my mind.
MARGARETA. Dear brother, this is agony!
VALENTINE. I tell you, let your weeping be!
    For when you cut yourself apart
    From honour, then you stabbed my heart.
    Now to the solemn sleep of death I go,
    An honest soldier, God receive me so.

CATHEDRAL NAVE

Service with organ and choir.
Margareta kneeling in the congregation; behind her an Evil Spirit.

EVIL SPIRIT. Ah, Gretchen, what a different girl
  Were you when with your innocent steps
  You came to face the altar here,
  And from your well-worn little book
  Murmured your prayers,
  Half in a childish pattern
  And half with a heart for God.
  Gretchen!
  How is it with your thoughts?
  And in your heart
  What deep transgression?
  Why pray you? Is it for your mother's soul,
  Sent by your hand to sleep in endless pain?
  Say, at your door whose blood is it?
    And just below your heart
  What is it stirs, already fluttering
  In boding anguish for itself and you?
MARGARETA. Dreadful, dreadful!
  If only I could shake it off,
  The thought that hovers all the time
  Against my will accusing me!
CHOIR. *Dies irae, dies illa*
  Solvet saeclum in favilla. (*Organ Music.*)
EVIL SPIRIT. Wrath hath thee now!
  The trumpet sounds,
  The graves are shaken.
  Now thy soul
  Is shaped anew,

From the cool dust
To pangs of flame,
New-born and quivering.

MARGARETA. Would I were gone from here!
The organ overwhelms me,
Crushes my breath,
My heart within me melting,
Lost in the flood of singing.

CHOIR. *Judex ergo cum sedebit,*
Quidquid latet adparebit,
Nil inultum remanebit.

MARGARETA. I feel so faint.
The very pillars
Close in upon me,
The vaulted roof
Comes crowding down.
Pray you, air!

EVIL SPIRIT. Thinkest to hide? Nay, sin and shame
Are never hidden.
Speakest of light and air?
Poor wretch!

CHOIR. *Quid sum miser tunc dicturus?*
Quem patronum rogaturus
Cum vix justus sit securus?

EVIL SPIRIT. From thee redeemed ones turn
Their countenance away.
The pure in heart now shudder
To reach a hand to thee,
Wretched, alas!

CHOIR. *Quid sum miser tunc dicturus?*

MARGARETA.
Neighbour – please – your phial. (*She swoons.*)

WALPURGIS NIGHT
(Mayday-Eve*)

In the Harz Mountains.
Faust. Mephistopheles.

MEPHISTOPHELES.
  You need a broomstick, Sir, to fly through space?
  Or a fierce goat I'd choose, of roughest breed:
  This road we trudge is nowhere near the place.
FAUST. While I feel fresh I like this walking pace,
  And then my black-thorn stick is all I need.
  What gain have we in shortening our ways?
  I love to thread the giant valleys' maze,
  Then climb the fell from whose majestic height
  The torrent falls in ceaseless silvery flight:
  Thus beauty gives the zest to travelling days.
  Already through the birches steals the spring,
  And even quivers soft in sombre firs,
  Shall not our limbs then feel the quickening?
MEPHISTOPHELES.
  In me, quite frankly, no such marvel stirs.
  I feel that winter reigns in my inside,
  Expecting here a trail of frost and snow.
  How sickly does the moon the heavens ride,
  With disc half-formed and reddish tardy glow,
  Her light so feeble that we hardly tread
  With safety through the dusky rocks and trees.
  I beg to call a will-o'-the-wisp instead:
  And there one is! Hi, you Sir, if you please!
  Your light could be to better purpose shed:
  We climb the hill, so kindly go ahead.

* It seems that a year has passed since the Eve that Mephistopheles mentions before the death of Valentine.

WILL-O'-THE-WISP.
>   In deep respect, I hope I may succeed,
>   And tame the natural lightness of my breed;
>   But custom sets a zig-zag to our course.

MEPHISTOPHELES.
>   So! Aping human creatures is his game?
>   Keep straight ahead, Sir, in the Devil's name,
>   Or else I'll snuff your candle at its source.

WILL-O'-THE-WISP.
>   The Master must be recognized perforce,
>   And willingly I'll do my best to please you,
>   But mind – bewitched is now the mountain-side,
>   And if your *Ignis fatuus* is your guide
>   'Tis not perfection that he guarantees you!

FAUST, MEPHISTOPHELES, WILL-O'-THE-WISP (*Antiphonal Trio*).
>   Now we wend our way, it seems,
>   Into witchery and dreams.
>   Prove your worth, good flickering guide,
>   Swiftly bringing us to glide
>   Through the vast and mournful spaces.
>   See, the pillared forest races
>   Tree on tree in vision reeling,
>   Cliffs that curtsey in their wheeling,
>   Snouted rocks in gulches roaring,
>   Hear their snarling and their snoring!
>   Through the rocks and meads come pouring
>   Brooks and rivers downward streaming.
>   Songs are these? In murmurs dreaming?
>   Airs are these of lovers' yearning,
>   Voices of the heavenly morning?
>   All we long for, hoping, aching!
>   Echo comes in power returning,

Legendary things redeeming.
    Uhoo! Shuhoo! floating over
Come the cries of owl and plover,
With the jay: they all are waking.
What are those, in thickets crawling?
Salamanders, belly-sprawling?
And the roots like wondrous snakes
Rise from rock and sandy soil,
Rise to fright us in the brakes,
Quick to catch us in a coil;
Knotted gnarls to catch at us
Wreathe their strands of polypus.
Fearful faring! And the swarming
Rodents run, their squadrons forming,
Black and blonde, through moss and heather,
While the glow-worms paint the weather,
In their crowded ranks providing
Crazy escort for our guiding.
    Nay, but tell me, in our traces
Are we standing or advancing?
All is whirling, swimming, dancing,
Fell and forest, full of faces,
Mock at us. The wild-fires, flying,
Menace in their multiplying.

MEPHISTOPHELES. Grip my coat and hold on tight!
    Here we reach a central height,
Where the mountain brings to view
Fires of Mammon shining through.

FAUST. Now glimmers vale and precipice
In strangest dawn, whose baleful glow
Lies lurid on the black abyss
And lights the chasms far below.
From pillared cloud or shredded vapours,

From veils of haze now comes the gleam,
Here to a slender scarf it tapers,
Here gushes forth a vivid stream;
Then threads of light in network surging
Their silver veins through valleys run,
Till, gathered by the hills converging,
The sundered filaments are one.
Now sparks burst blossoming near at hand
Like scattered fire of golden sand,
And now in looming stature, lo,
The wall of rock is all aglow.

MEPHISTOPHELES. Lord Mammon's liberality invests
His palace with a wealth of festal light.
Lucky for you that you have seen the sight;
And now I scent his wanton hurtling guests.

FAUST.
How fierce the storm-bride's forces swoop and hiss,
And with what buffets beat my neck and shoulders.

MEPHISTOPHELES.
Clasp then the cliff's old ribs! Cling to the boulders!
Or else she hurls you to the deep abyss.
Night now wears a misty hood.
Hark to the crashing in the wood!
Owls affrighted swerve and shriek,
Greenwood takes the tempest's lash,
Pillared giants split and crash
Where the storms their wreckage wreak.
Root and bole are groaning, straining,
In the forest's huge complaining.
Riot rends the tree-tops, all
Madly mingle, crack or fall.
Through the havoc-littered gorges
Howl the wind's unpitying scourges.

Walpurgis Night

    Voices in the height you hear,
    Distant now or sounding near,
    Streaming through the mountain range,
    Magic chanting, maddening, strange.

WITCHES IN CHORUS.
    Now to the Brocken the witches ride;
    The stubble is gold and the corn is green;
    There is the carnival crew to be seen,
    And Squire Urianus will come to preside.
    So over the valleys our company floats,
    With witches a-farting on stinking old goats.

A VOICE. The venerable Baubo now
    Comes riding on her farrow-sow.

CHORUS.
    Then honour be where honour's due:
    Dame Baubo up, and lead the crew!
    With a tough old sow, a mother as well,
    She'd marshal witches or shades of hell.

A VOICE. Which way have you come?
ANOTHER VOICE.   By Ilsen-stone.
    Looked in on the owl, where she roosted alone.
    I tell you, her eyes
    Were big with surprise.

VOICE. To hell with you! Why do you need
    To ride such a speed?

ANOTHER VOICE. See, her foul riding bored me!
    Wounds she has scored me
    And gored me!

CHORUS OF WITCHES.
    The way is long, the way is broad,
    Whence comes the frantic weltering horde?
    Broom can scratch and prong can poke,
    The womb may burst and the infant choke.

SEMI-CHORUS OF WARLOCKS.
>   We travel like the house-bound snail,
>   With dames far ahead, and us at the tail.
>   For, if in evil you compete,
>   Dames have a start of a thousand feet.

SECOND SEMI-CHORUS.
>   This we endure without much fuss:
>   Though women may outdistance us,
>   What shall their thousand feet avail?
>   In one good jump arrives the male.

VOICE (*from above*).
>   Come with us, come, from Felsenmere!

VOICES (*from below*).
>   Could we but join your lofty sphere!
>   Though we may wash us free from stain,
>   Blighted and barren we remain.

DOUBLE CHORUS.
>   The winds are hushed, the stars are pale,
>   The mournful moon puts on her veil.
>   In wild career the witches' choir
>   Scatters a thousand sparks of fire.

VOICES (*from below*). Stay, stay! You shall not pass!

VOICE (*from above*).
>   Who calls there, from the dark crevasse?

VOICE (*from below*). Ah, take me with you, take me, pray!
>   Three hundred years I climb this way,
>   And never gain the magic peak,
>   Nor find the kith and kin I seek.

DOUBLE CHORUS.
>   Broom will bear and stick will lift,
>   Pitch-fork and he-goat have the gift;
>   And he who cannot rise to-day
>   Is damned and doomed in his dismay.

Walpurgis Night

DEMI-WITCH (*below*). I hobble up, a plaguey time,
   And all outstrip me in the climb.
   At home I have disquiet and fear,
   And, blast it, do no better here.
CHORUS OF WITCHES.
   Here's ointment if your courage fails,
   And clouts and rags will serve for sails.
   A trough's the vessel for your flight:
   She's damned who cannot fly to-night!
DOUBLE CHORUS. And when we sail around the top
   First skim the ground, then fill it up,
   That all the Brocken height may be
   Smothered in swarms of witchery.
            (*They alight.*)
MEPHISTOPHELES.
   Here's shoving, bustling, crowding, clattering,
   Whizzing and squirming, flitting, chattering,
   With singeing spark and stink and speed,
   True product of the witches breed!
   Keep close, lest we be parted. Sir, take heed!
   Where are you now?
FAUST.   Here!
MEPHISTOPHELES.   So far from your course?
   Then must I exercise patronal force.
   Make way! Squire Voland comes. Sweet scum, make way!
   Now, Doctor, not a moment more to stay!
   Hold fast my cloak! We vanish, and are free:
   This orgy even shocks the likes of me.
   Besides, yon spinney gleams with curious light,
   Come, let us steal upon its mystery:
   Duck in the thicket, and we're out of sight.
FAUST. Then lead, perverse and contradictory Sprite,

And brilliant is the plan you have pursued:
We climb the Brocken on Walpurgis Night
To cultivate our love of solitude.

MEPHISTOPHELES.
But see, those lively lights among the heather,
A small congenial club is met together,
And solitude is cheered with company.

FAUST. Yet on the upland I would rather be,
Where glowing fires begin and whirls of smoke.
The Soul of Evil dominates the folk,
And surely many riddles will be solved.

MEPHISTOPHELES.
And new ones, just as puzzling, evolved.
I tell you, let the world's mad traffic be,
While here we sit in quiet security.
Indeed it is proverbially true,
From greater worlds we fashion small ones too:
Witches I see stark naked, Sir, and young,
And old ones, who do well to veil their charms.
For my sake show a courteous eye and tongue:
Much sport with little trouble – why have qualms?
Now comes the sound of many an instrument –
A cursèd din, but custom gives consent!
Come, Sir, with me! No sooner said than done,
I'll take the lead and guide you to the fun,
And earn your gratitude in recompense.
What do you say? No petty realm is this.
Lift up your eyes! The prospect is immense:
A hundred fires now circle the abyss.
They chatter, dance, brew, drink, have love's caress;
A scene 'twere hard to beat, you must confess.

FAUST. But when you introduce us at the revel,
Shall you appear as sorcerer, or devil?

Walpurgis Night

MEPHISTOPHELES. Though I am used to go incognito,
  On gala-days one's Orders ought to show.
  My rank requires no garter for its proof,
  But folk will honour here the cloven hoof.
  D'you see yon snail, comes creeping up to me?
  She, with her groping sensitive face,
  Has caught a whiff of my dark majesty:
  I cannot hide from this my populace.
  But come, of all these fires we'll make the tour:
  I'll be the pander, you can be the wooer.
      (*To some who sit around the dying embers.*)
  Why sit aloof, old club-men, in the gloam?
  Far better come
  Where there is joy and riot;
  There, with the whirl of youth around you,
  I would have found you;
  Surely you have enough of quiet
  When you're at home.

GENERAL.
  The Nations? Never trust 'em – always trimmin',
  You get no thanks, however much you serve.
  The People, Sir, they're just the same as women,
  Their favours go to youth, without reserve.

MINISTER. Our decadence from Right I must deplore:
  The men of old were certainly more sage,
  For when the word of ministers was law,
  Then was, beyond a doubt, the Golden Age.

PROFITEER. And we, by no means lacking in our wits,
  Have pushed ahead ignoring right and wrong.
  And now things waltz around and fall to bits,
  Just when we thought our situation strong.

AUTHOR. Who wants to read, pray tell me, nowadays
  A book that has a modicum of meaning?

As for the younger generation's ways,
They never were so pert and overweening!

MEPHISTOPHELES (*suddenly appearing senile*).
Seeing this Brocken-trip may be my last,
I know the nation's day of doom is nigh;
And since my little cask is running dry,
The universe is surely sinking fast.

HUCKSTER-WITCH. Kind gentlemen, don't pass me by
Without a look at my display.
There's curious items on my tray
The rarest taste to satisfy.
What's more, there's nothing in my shop,
Whose store all other shops exceeds,
That has not added to the crop
Of worldly ills and evil deeds.
No dagger here that has not dripped with blood,
No chalice but has held a lethal juice
To blight a life of promise in the bud,
No pearl but served a maiden to seduce,
No sword but served a traitor's foul attack
Or stabbed a strong opponent in the back.

MEPHISTOPHELES. Gammer, your stuff is out of date;
Time flies, and what is past is done.
Try novelties for salesman's bait,
For novelty wins everyone.

FAUST. This, with a vengeance, is a Witches' Fete.
I fear lest sense and reason abdicate.

MEPHISTOPHELES.
The whirling mob swarms to the heights above
And shoves you with it, when yourself would shove.

FAUST. But who comes here?

MEPHISTOPHELES.   'Tis Lilith.

FAUST.   Who?

Walpurgis Night

MEPHISTOPHELES. Ay, she,
First wife to Adam, mark her carefully,
Her, Lilith, with her dangerous lovely tresses.
Of this, her sole adornment, best beware,
For virile youth, when taken in that snare,
Will come not lightly off from her caresses.

FAUST.
There's a young witch, paired with one old and bowed:
They've danced like mad, and look for some release.

MEPHISTOPHELES. To-day there is no sort of peace.
Another dance strikes up. Come, join the crowd!

FAUST (*dancing with the young witch*).
Once on a day I had a dream:
An apple-tree was my delight.
I saw two lovely apples gleam,
And climbed, with rising appetite.

THE FAIR ONE. The pretty fruit has tempted you
Since first in Paradise it grew;
And I confess, with heart aglow,
Those apples in my garden grow.

MEPHISTOPHELES (*dancing with the old witch*).
Once on a day I had a dream,
With wanton horticultural theme:
A monstrous gash was on a tree;
Wide though it was, it suited me.

THE OLD ONE. With deep respect I here salute
His Lordship of the cloven foot:
Let him provide a sturdy pole
And not be frightened of the hole.

SIR RUNIC RUMP.*
Accursèd race, up to your tricks again!
How often have we proved, beyond disputing,

---
* See Introduction, p. 23.

No ghost can stand upon a normal footing?
And yet you dare to dance like mortal men!
THE FAIR ONE (*dancing*).
What is this person doing at our fair?
FAUST. Why, bless your life, the fellow's everywhere.
Others may dance but he awards the prize,
No single turn, but he must criticize:
If you so much as step without his word,
Then, please agree, that step has not occurred.
His fury rises most if we advance:
Go round in circles, in frustrated dance –
Just as our critic will,
Turning his rusty mill –
And then he'll say you move with style and sense,
Especially if you hail his influence.
SIR RUNIC RUMP.
Impertinence! The sprites intend to stay!
Be off with you, you've been explained away!
By rules this devil's-crew is nothing daunted:
For all our wisdom, Tegel* still is haunted.
Long have I toiled to purge this madness hence,
And still it clings, with sheer impertinence!
THE FAIR ONE.
Then cease your babble: we have had enough.
SIR RUNIC RUMP.
I tell you plain, you and your witches' schism,
I'll not endure this spirit-despotism,
My spirit cannot dominate such stuff.
(*The dance goes on.*)
As for to-day, my plans have gone askew;
Yet where the witches travel I'll attend,
And hope, before I reach the very end,

---

* See Introduction, p. 23.

All devils and all poets to subdue.

MEPHISTOPHELES.
To seek relief he now sits in a puddle,
For by this method he is much improved;
And when the leeches on his backside huddle
His phantoms and his wits are both removed.
    (*To Faust, who has left the dance.*)
Why do you leave your lovely singing girl,
The sweetest prize of this night's partnerships?

FAUST. Oh! Even as she sang
    There sprang
A little mouse of crimson from her lips.

MEPHISTOPHELES. A trifle, Sir! Your lip might curl
Had he been grey. Pretend no pang,
    Or chaste harangue,
On such a night of longing, when
We yield ourselves in love's sicilienne.

FAUST. And then I saw –
MEPHISTOPHELES.   What, then?
FAUST.   Mephisto, see you where
There stands a girl unfriended, pale and fair?
She slowly turns, and moves with steps of pain,
And, as I live, I think I recognize
My loving Gretchen, there before my eyes.

MEPHISTOPHELES.
Let that alone! Such thoughts can do no good.
This is a witchery, a phantom, dead;
To meet with it is luckless, full of dread,
Its frigid stare congeals the gazer's blood,
Till stony death through all the limbs is spread –
Of the Medusa, Sir, you must have read.

FAUST. Indeed, indeed, the eyes are of the dead,
Eyes that no hand has closed or comforted.

That bosom Gretchen yielded, lovely, warm,
 I took my joy of that dear, gentle form.
MEPHISTOPHELES.
 That is the witch-craft, poor deluded fool:
 Each sees in her the sweetheart of his soul.
FAUST. What longing love, what ecstasy and woe!
 This haunting gaze will never let me go,
 And strangely clear, around her lovely throat,
 She has a single cord of red,
 Thin as a knife-blade is the thread.
MEPHISTOPHELES. Correct, a detail I myself now note.
 Under her arm she sometimes bears her head,
 Cut by the blow the gallant Perseus smote.
 But I perceive you dote on phantoms still;
 Then please accompany me to yonder hill,
 Vienna has no gaiety more fair;
 If not deceived, I see a theatre there.
 What is the piece?
SERVIBILIS. A thing we now prepare,
 A novelty, the seventh of its kind,
 The product of a dilettante mind;
 Plays sevenfold the public here prefers,
 And all the actors, Sir, are amateurs.
 Pardon, your worships, if I disappear:
 As amateur I draw the curtain here.
MEPHISTOPHELES.
 'Midst madness on the Blocksberg, it is clear,
 You amateurs are in your proper sphere.

WALPURGIS NIGHT'S DREAM

OR THE GOLDEN WEDDING OF OBERON AND TITANIA

A Lyrical Intermezzo*

STAGE MANAGER. As to the scenery for our tale,
  Rest, good sons of Mieding*:
  Hoary hill and misty vale
  Are all we shall be needing.
HERALD. Marriage needs its fifty years
  To claim the golden title:
  The quarrel done, that raised our fears,
  Gold is a glad requital.
OBERON. Are you near me, spirit train,
  Then grace our celebration;
  King and Queen are met again
  In love's new coronation.
PUCK. Puck arrives and quickly shows
  A pretty leg at dancing,
  And hundreds follow where he goes,
  With smiling joy advancing.
ARIEL. Ariel now sends showers of song
  And wondrous sweet his lute is;
  His music summons drolls along,
  But also brings the beauties.
OBERON. Wedded couples, seeking bliss,
  Let example guide you.
  The recipe for love is this,
  That first we must divide you.
TITANIA. He sulks, or she capricious grows:
  Seize them, as their dictator!

* See Introduction, p. 23.

Send sulky to the Arctic snows
And her to the Equator!
ORCHESTRA TUTTI (*fortissimo*).
Nose of fly and snout of midge,
And kindred apparitions,
Cricket in grass and frog in sedge,
These same are our musicians.
SOLO. Sweetly now the bagpipe blows,
A bubble for his sack.
Hear him, down his snubby nose,
Play snecker-snicker-snack.
EMBRYO SPIRIT. Give winglets for the puny beast,
And spider's foot and paunch of toad:
If not an animal, at least
It may turn out a little ode.
A TINY COUPLE. Lofty leap and mincing step,
In dew and scented briar:
Though very daintily you trip,
The feet can fly no higher.
INQUISITIVE TRAVELLER.
I dream a dream within this glade,
A drunken or a sober one:
Is it my luck in masquerade
To meet the fair god Oberon?
ORTHODOX. No claws he has, and no tail-piece,
Yet he, to judge this revel,
Must, like the pagan gods of Greece,
Be classified as devil.
ARTIST FROM THE NORTH.
My present canvases, I know,
Are little more than sketches,
But on a journey I shall go,
To see what Italy teaches.

Walpurgis Night's Dream

STICKLER. This masquerade unluckily
  Grows bawdier and louder:
  Of all the witches that I see
  There's only two wear powder.
YOUNG WITCH. Powder you need, or petticoat,
  For matrons old and shoddy;
  But I sit naked on my goat
  To show my lusty body.
MATRON. Our manners are too good, my dear,
  To match a youthful scolder,
  I merely hope the time is near
  When you will rot and moulder.
CONDUCTOR. Snout of fly and trump of midge,
  Spare her, so nude and sweet, Sirs!
  And cricket too, and frog in sedge –
  And pray observe the beat, Sirs.
WEATHERCOCK (*turning to one side*).
  Here's company diverse and gay,
  With brides and their relations,
  And bachelors in good array
  With ardent expectations.
WEATHERCOCK (*turning to the other side*).
  And should the crust of earth not gape
  To swallow up this revel,
  I'll look to hell for my escape
  And dive down to the devil.
XENIA. With little spears, and sharp they are,
  We insects come a-flitting,
  Satan our reverend papa
  To honour as is fitting.
HENNINGS.* See them, in their teeming swarm,
  Bringing jibes so artless,
  They'll tell us next they mean no harm,

---

* See Introduction, page 23

    And not to think them heartless.
MUSAGETES. To dwell among this witches'-crew
    My spirit gladly chooses:
    I'd rather have with them to do
    Than try to lead the Muses.
CI-DEVANT GENIUS OF THE AGE.
    Hitch on to me, choose friends aright,
    And no-one can surpass us,
    For roomy is the Blocksberg's height,
    Like 'Germany's Parnassus'.
INQUISITIVE TRAVELLER.
    Say, who is yonder pompous man
    Who steps with haughty paces?
    He sniffs and snuffles all he can
    Upon the Jesuits' traces.
CRANE. Though fishing's fair in lucid lakes,
    There's sport in troubled waters;
    And so your pious soul betakes
    Himself to devil's quarters.
A SON OF THE WORLD.
    The pious, Sir, regard all means
    As blessedly authentical;
    And so their piety convenes
    On Blocksberg its conventicle.
DANCER. A new choir now its wings will fledge,
    I hear a distant drumming.
    Nay, 'tis the bitterns in the sedge
    With sad, monotonous thrumming.
BALLET-MASTER. Come fat and thin to shake their legs
    And ape the dancer's motion.
    Of how they move their clumsy pegs,
    They've not the faintest notion.
FIDDLER. These scurvy gangs will love their feasts,

Walpurgis Night's Dream

When murder would delight them;
If Orpheus with his lute led beasts,
The bagpipes here unite them.

DOGMATIST. They shout me deaf, but I insist,
'Gainst critics and their cavils,
The Devil must in fact exist,
Or how could there be devils?

IDEALIST. Ideas can be a tyranny
To give one mental twinges:
If all my thoughts are really me,
My mind is off its hinges.

REALIST. Ontology will drive me mad,
Its mazes are nefarious.
My outlook never was so bad,
My footing is precarious.

SUPERNATURALIST. With much delight I join this crew
And share with them the revels,
Proving the virtuous spirits true
By studying the devils.

SCEPTIC. They rake for gold in flame and grime,
And think they track the treasure;
But 'cavil' will with 'devil' rhyme,
And that I do with pleasure.

CONDUCTOR. Cricket shrill and frog in sedge,
You amateur musicians:
Snout of fly and trump of midge,
What damnable emissions!

CLEVER ONES. Amusement's regiment are we,
Sans-Souci's leading models.
Our feet have suffered atrophy,
So we walk on our noddles.

THE UNSKILLED.
We've scrounged good victuals in our day,

God help us, that is done with!
And, now our shoes are worn away,
Bare feet are all we run with.

WILL-O'-THE-WISPS. From the marshes we advance,
To show our tricky talents,
And find that when we join the dance
We shine as super-gallants.

SHOOTING-STAR. Through the glints of stars I pass,
Fierily down-shooting.
Now I sprawl, deep in the grass,
Help me to my footing!

HEAVYWEIGHTS. Here we come, make way, make way!
Deep grasses we will trample,
And prove that spirits can display
Good solid limbs and ample.

PUCK. Elephants would make less noise
When their mother bellows.
Plumpest here to-day, my boys,
Is Puck, the best of fellows.

ARIEL. Does fair Nature give you wings,
Wings that the soul discloses?
Follow where your Ariel sings,
On paths and hills of roses.

ORCHESTRA (*pianissimo*). Clouds go by and mists recede,
Bathed in the dawn and blended;
Sighs the wind in leaf and reed,
And all our tale is ended.

DESOLATE DAY
IN OPEN COUNTRY

Faust. Mephistopheles.

FAUST. In misery and deep despair! Long, long a piteous wanderer upon the earth, and now to be trapped! Cast into prison, she, that lovely creature, unhappiest of souls, in fearful torment, a felon! Is it then come to this?

Treacherous, ignoble Spirit, this you kept concealed from me. And now will you stand, stand and glare in your devilish wrath, rolling your hateful eyes, stand and affront me with your unbearable presence? A prisoner, in wretchedness irreparable, delivered over to spirits of evil, and to the judgment of harsh, censorious men. And me meanwhile you lull with banal dissipations, hide from me her mounting misery, and leave her to go lonely and helpless to her ruin.

MEPHISTOPHELES. She is not the first.

FAUST. Hell-hound! Abominable monster! Look down, O infinite Spirit, and turn this reptile once more to the likeness of a cur, the shape in which he was pleased to scamper ahead of me in the night, rolling at the feet of the innocent wayfarer or bestriding his shoulders if he fell. Change him once more to the stature that he loves, that he may crawl before me on his belly in the dirt, till I spurn the despicable creature with my foot.

Not the first! Misery and woe, deeper than a human soul can fathom, that more than one poor being should be whelmed in this swamp of wretchedness; that one first victim could not atone for the guilt of all others by its agony of suffering, in the sight of the Eternal Forgiver! The anguish of this one soul strikes me to the very heart, while you grin coolly at the fate of thousands!

MEPHISTOPHELES. So here we are, at the uttermost bounds of understanding – that is to say, where the wit of man breaks down. Why did you throw in your lot with ours if you cannot stay the course? Fly, will you, you who are apt to turn giddy? Was it we who forced our way to you, or you who thrust yourself on us?

FAUST. Do not gnash your greedy teeth at me! You fill me with disgust.

Great and glorious Spirit, whose countenance was vouchsafed to me, Thou who knowest my very heart and soul, why must I be fettered to this infamous companion, who battens upon mischief and delights in ruin?

MEPHISTOPHELES. Have you finished?

FAUST. Save her, I tell you, or it shall go hard with you. The most fearful curse upon you, through aeons of time.

MEPHISTOPHELES. It is not for me to lay off the bonds of the Avenger, nor to draw back his bolts. Save her, you say! Who was it sent her to her ruin, I or you? (*Faust looks around him with a wild despair.*) Think you to wield the thunderbolt? Luckily that power was not granted to you miserable mortals. To crush the innocent thing that crosses you, there lies your true tyrant's way of ending your embarrassments.

FAUST. Lead me to her! She shall be free!

MEPHISTOPHELES. What of the danger to which you then expose yourself? In this town, remember, there is still a hue and cry for the blood spilt by your hand. Over the death-place of a creature slain, hover avenging spirits, waiting for the return of the murderer.

FAUST. You dare to say that to me? May there fall upon you, monster, the death and murder of a whole world! Lead me where she is, I tell you, and set her free!

MEPHISTOPHELES. I will be your guide, so hear now what

I can do. Is all the power of heaven and earth in my keeping? I will lay a cloud upon the senses of her gaoler. I will make you master of the keys, and bring her forth by the power of a human hand. I will keep watch, the horses are ready, and I will bear you away. This is in my power.
FAUST. Up and away!

NIGHT, OPEN COUNTRY

Faust, Mephistopheles, mounted upon black horses, in furious gallop.

FAUST.
 What things are they weaving on Gallows-hill?
MEPHISTOPHELES.
 Their brewing and doing is nobody's knowing.
FAUST. Swooping, ascending, bowing and bending.
MEPHISTOPHELES. A guild of witches.
FAUST. They make libation and consecration.
MEPHISTOPHELES. On, and away.

PRISON

FAUST (*before an iron door, with keys and a light*).
 With long-forgotten woe my spirit groans,
 I shudder at the load of mortal ill.
 Here she is lodged, behind these clammy stones,
 And all her crime an innocent blind will.
 You shrink to seek her in this place,
 You fear to meet her face to face!
 Delay not! Else may death his doom fulfil.
  (*He seizes the lock. There is a sound of singing within.*)

MARGARETA (*from within*). My mother, the drab,
  She did me to death,
  My father, the villain,
  Devoured me in wrath.
  My sister so small
  Had my bones one and all
  In the cool to lay.
  Now I have heard,
  Changed to a bird,
  The woodland call,
  To fly far away.
FAUST (*unlocking the door*).
  Little she dreams her lover, at her door,
  Can hear the jangling chains and rustling straw.
        (*He goes in.*)
MARGARETA (*cowering upon her pallet*).
  Alas, they come! Death, bitter death is near!
FAUST. I come to set you free. Speak softly, dear!
MARGARETA.
  Can you not pity? Have you not human eyes?
FAUST. Love, you will wake the gaoler with your cries.
    (*He takes hold of her chains to set her free. She kneels.*)
MARGARETA. How come I, hangman, in your power?
  Whose was the fatal word to give?
  You fetch me at the midnight hour.
  Have pity, let me live!
  Soon comes the morning, when the knell is rung,
  To take my living breath, (*She rises.*)
  And I so young, so very young.
  And fair I was, and that has been my death.
  My lover was so close, now he is gone.
  My flowers are torn, my garlands trampled on.
  Your hands upon me are so rough and strong.

Prison 191

    Spare me this force, I never did you wrong;
    So, be not deaf to what I now implore,
    I never saw you in my life before.
FAUST. Be still, my tears, lest like a coward I shrink.
MARGARETA. Now I am yours, without defence.
    Let me first give my babe to drink.
    All night I nursed its innocence;
    They took it from me, out of spite, I think,
    And say I killed it, in their insolence,
    And evermore my misery will grow.
    The folk make me their song, cruel, overweening;
    I knew a ballad once that ended so —
    Who gave them leave to turn it to this meaning?
FAUST (*throwing himself upon his knees*).
    Here at your feet I kneel, your loving friend,
    The fetters of this misery to rend.
MARGARETA (*falling on her knees at his side*).
    Yes, let us kneel and beg the Saints to hear!
    The threshold flickers, glares,
    And in the solid stairs
    Seethings of hell appear.
    Satan is near,
    The shrieking, grim
    And hideous brim
    Of Hell to uncover.
FAUST (*in a loud voice*). Gretchen! Gretchen!
MARGARETA (*attentively*). That was the voice of my lover.
    (*She leaps to her feet, and the chains fall from her.*)
    Where can he be? I heard him call,
    And I am free, my fetters fall.
    I'll clasp him to me, and none shall stay me,
    And on his bosom I will lay me.
    He called me 'Gretchen'. He stood at my door

In the midst of the hellish clatter and roar;
Cleaving the din and the devilish scorn
The sweet loved voice of my lover was borne.

FAUST. I am he!

MARGARETA. You are he! Oh, tell me once again!
(She embraces him.)
Ah, it is he! And I am loosed from pain.
Where are the dungeon's fears, the chains they gave me?
Dear, it is you, you who have come to save me.
And I am saved!
And now I see the street before me yet,
The street where first we met,
The garden gay with flowers, and the gate
Where, for your coming, Martha and I would wait.

FAUST. Come, come with me!

MARGARETA. Oh, linger here!
I gladly linger, love, when you are near.

FAUST. Away!
Risk no delay!
Our only hope is this,
And sadly shall we rue it if we miss.

MARGARETA. How so, dear love? Do you no longer kiss?
A little time, the waning of a moon,
And is the kiss of love unlearnt so soon?
Why, clinging to your breast, have I this fear,
When once your words, your dear eyes gazing down,
Would lift my soul as to another sphere,
And you would kiss me till I thought to drown.
Kiss me now,
Else I kiss you.
Alas, alas! Your lips are chill
And dumb!
What is of true-love become?

Who has done me this ill?
  (*She turns away from him.*)
FAUST. Come, follow me, dear heart! Be bold,
And I will give you love a thousandfold;
But follow me, love, this I beg of you!
MARGARETA.
And is it you indeed? Can this be true?
FAUST. 'Tis I. Dear, come!
MARGARETA. You freed me from my chain,
Indeed you took me to your heart again;
How comes it that you have no dread of me?
Or know you not the creature that you free?
FAUST. Nay, come!
Dawn softens night, the deepest shades are fled.
MARGARETA. My mother, by my hand, lies dead;
Dead is my child, that I did drown.
Was it not sent to be our own?
Yours, too. – 'Tis you, so strange though it may seem.
Give me your hand. See, this is not a dream.
Your own dear hand – but, oh, a reeking hand!
Come, wipe it dry! For, as I understand,
'Tis blood that makes it wet.
Dear God! What have you done amiss?
Cover your dagger's threat,
I do beseech you this!
FAUST. Let the past be! The terrors it will start!
Dear, you will break my heart.
MARGARETA. Ah no, I die, but you must live;
Then listen to the reckoning I give
Of graves you must prepare;
Even to-morrow, tend them, love, with care.
In the best place my mother shall abide,
And then my brother, by her side.

    Me, lay
    Some space apart – yet not too far away.
    And lay my little child to my right breast:
    No other soul there is with me to rest.
    I nestled to your side in times now gone;
    That was a joy, a bliss to dream upon.
    And now that joy will nevermore come true;
    As if you shut me from your heart and mind,
    I strangely seem to force my way to you.
    And yet you stand before me, good and kind.
FAUST. If in your heart you see your lover near,
    Come, there is nothing that we may not dare.
MARGARETA. To go from here?
FAUST. To freedom.
MARGARETA. If my grave is there,
    And death has vigil there to keep,
    Come, I will go to endless sleep,
    Else, not a footstep may I move;
    And so,
    You turn to go? –
    If only I could come, Heinrich, my love!
FAUST. Only take heart! Unbolted is the door.
MARGARETA.
    I must remain, for hope is mine no more.
    How shall flight help me? Still they lie in wait.
    A wretched life, to beg one's bread,
    And worse when conscience bears an evil dread.
    To roam far lands is sad, without a friend;
    And they will catch me in the end.
FAUST. I will not leave you.
MARGARETA. Quickly, quickly,
    Save your child!
    Follow the way

Prison

    Down by the brook,
    There, by the foot-bridge,
    Look,
    Left of the wood,
    Where stood
    The rail and the plank,
    There, in the pool,
    Quickly, your hand!
    It gropes for the bank,
    With fluttering limbs,
    Save it, oh, save it!
FAUST. Calm yourself, dear,
    A single step, and you are free from fear.
MARGARETA. Past the hill and far from here,
    If only we were past and gone!
    My mother sits on yonder stone.
    A breath of ice is in my hair.
    My mother sits on yonder stone,
    And shakes her head, in her despair.
    She beckons not, nor nods to me,
    Her head moves slowly, heavily.
    So deep her sleep, she never more will wake.
    She slumbered for our passion's sake,
    And so much joy was ours to take,
    Such happiness to share.
FAUST. To dare,
    Were better here than to beseech!
    My arms you shall find stronger than my speech.
MARGARETA.
    I will not yield to force! Let me alone!
    Nay, come not near me with your murderous reach,
    When all my love I gave you as your own.
FAUST. Dear heart, dear heart, now breaks the day.

MARGARETA.
>   Day, yes, the day; the last dread day breaks in.
>   My wedding-day, it should have been.
>   Tell not a soul you were in Gretchen's room.
>   My wreath was twined with pain,
>   So ran the fatal chance.
>   We two shall meet again,
>   But never again in the dance.
>   They crowd upon me, hosts on noiseless feet;
>   Alley and square and street
>   Such legions scarce can hold.
>   Snapped is the wand, the knell of guilt is tolled,
>   They seize me, they bind me with lashes,
>   On the scaffold I stand alone,
>   The crowd gazes up on high,
>   Each feeling the keen edge nigh,
>   As if my throat were his own.
>   The sharp steel flashes.
>   The world lies mute as a stone.

FAUST. Would I had never been born!

MEPHISTOPHELES (*appearing without*).
>   Lost are you both if you stay.
>   Can you not see it is morn?
>   Away!
>   You haver and chatter yet,
>   While my horses tremble and sweat.
>   Wherefore delay?
>   The dawn grows bright.

MARGARETA. What evil thing has risen from the ground?
>   He, ah, not he! – Forbid him from my sight!
>   On holy ground he has no right,
>   He wants my soul, to torture and confound,
>   He waits my death.

Prison 197

FAUST. Nay, you shall live.
MARGARETA.
   Into God's hand my trembling soul I give.
MEPHISTOPHELES (*to Faust*).
   Come, or I let you share her wretched end.
MARGARETA.
   Lord, I am thine, oh, save me and defend!
   Father, let angels now have charge of me,
   Encamped around in heavenly company.
   Heinrich, I have a dread of thee.
MEPHISTOPHELES. She is condemned to die.
A VOICE (*from above*). Is redeemed on high.
MEPHISTOPHELES (*to Faust*). Hither, to me!
          (*He vanishes, with Faust.*)
VOICE (*from within, dying away*). Heinrich! Heinrich!

*The following pages
describe other volumes in
the Penguin Classics
series*

GOETHE

FAUST: PART TWO

Translated by Philip Wayne

This translation of the second part completes Philip Wayne's translation of Goethe's *Faust* for the Penguin Classics. In Part One Goethe gave the world the famous human myth that embodied love and devilment and longing aspiration. In the second part he brings the constantly striving Faust through the utmost reaches of human speculation to a salvation evoking the most profound poetic compassion.

DOSTOYEVSKY

CRIME AND PUNISHMENT

Translated by David Magarshack

When he began, in 1865, to write *Crime and Punishment*, the great novel which extended his reputation outside Russia, Dostoyevsky himself was as embarrassed with debts as Raskolnikov, the young student who, in the book, murders a stupid and grasping old woman for gain. In Raskolnikov's inability to tolerate his growing sense of guilt the author handles a universal theme on which he had brooded during his imprisonment in Siberia.

The reader of David Magarshack's fluent translation can appreciate both a magnificent gallery of characters and that piercing insight which makes Dostoyevsky the most terrifying of all writers.

DOSTOYEVSKY

THE BROTHERS KARAMAZOV

Translated by David Magarshack

The Brothers Karamazov, the culmination of Dostoyevsky's work, was completed in 1880, shortly before his death. A simple story of parricide and fraternal jealousy profoundly involves the questions of anarchism, atheism, and the existence of God.

The first volume in David Magarshack's excellent modern translation introduces Fyodor Karamazov, a mean and disreputable Russian land-owner, and his three legitimate sons: Dmitry, a profligate army officer; Ivan, a writer with revolutionary ideas; and Alexey, a religious novice. They meet to resolve a family dispute in the presence of the elder, Zossima.

In the second volume Dmitry Karamazov is apprehended at the height of a wild orgy with his mistress and charged with the murder of his father, who has been robbed and killed by night. At the subsequent trial Ivan, his brother, throws the court into confusion, and the verdict which follows carries little conviction.

DOSTOYEVSKY

THE DEVILS

Translated by David Magarshack

Published eighty years ago, *The Devils*, which ranks next to *Crime and Punishment* and *The Idiot* among Dostoyevsky's best-known masterpieces, has provoked more controversy and passion than any other Dostoyevsky novel. Hailed by some as an exposure of Communism and denounced by others as the work of a reactionary renegade, *The Devils* still holds the stage as an exciting and stimulating commentary on men and affairs, on politics and religion, on the dark passions of the human heart, and the strange and miraculous transformations wrought in it by pity and understanding. The novel is a political melodrama, ending in a shambles that can only be compared with the ending of *Hamlet*. To the unprejudiced mind, however, it contains a great deal of sound insight into modern politics, some malicious caricatures of revolutionaries and literary personalities (such as Turgenev), and a wealth of all sorts of odd, but strangely human, characters.

DOSTOYEVSKY

THE IDIOT

Translated by David Magarshack

The Idiot, which Dostoyevsky wrote after *Crime and Punishment*, is his most absorbing and structurally perfect masterpiece. In it he deals brilliantly with the position of the good, saintly man in modern society and the question whether such a man can survive in a world torn by human passions. Love, the main theme of the novel, is considered in three different ways: love based on passion, love from vanity, and Christian love. The hero of the novel, Prince Myshkin, a Christ-like figure, becomes deeply involved in the clash of contending passions and his attempts to reconcile them end in disaster and tragedy.

Dostoyevsky's uncanny insight into the motives of human behaviour, his wonderful artistic integration of idea and character, and his uncompromising truth to life combine to make *The Idiot* one of the finest examples of the psychological novel in European literature.

TOLSTOY

ANNA KARENIN

Translated by Rosemary Edmonds

Tolstoy began to write *Anna Karenin* in 1875, six years after he had finished *War and Peace*, and it is considered by many to be the greater of the two. It is the story of Anna, one of the most admired women of fashionable Moscow and St Petersburg society, who gives up her husband, her son, and her position for a passion which finally drives her to suicide. And in contrast there is the story of Levin, which reflects the apparent peace of Tolstoy's own marriage. On the surface he lives a happy and contented country existence, and yet within is tormented by an intense need to discover the meaning of life without which he can see no purpose in living. In the end this is revealed to him by the simple words of a peasant – a conclusion which mitigates the horror of Anna's death.

TOLSTOY

WAR AND PEACE

Translated by Rosemary Edmonds

Although Tolstoy started work on *War and Peace* 'excited by the idea of writing a psychological novel of Alexander and Napoleon, and of all the baseness, all the empty phrases, the foolishness and the inconsistencies of their *entourage* and of the pair themselves', his subject was really humanity. The brilliantly portrayed historical tableaux are used as a foil and background for the personal dramas of those who took part in them: it is always the effect of an event on the individual which interested Tolstoy, not the event itself. But as well as giving us all the 'superbly rendered domesticity', over which Arnold Bennett was so enthusiastic, and the realism of the Battle scenes, Tolstoy comes forward as the philosopher and moralist, and may be identified with the two heroes, Pierre Bezuhov and Prince Andrei, in their strivings towards the eternal and the absolute. His message is that the only fundamental obligation of man is to be true to life. *War and Peace* is both a hymn to life and a magnificent analysis of the Russian nation during one of its most critical periods. 'When the Russian Empire ceases to exist, new generations will turn to *War and Peace* to find out what sort of people were the Russians.'

Also available

CHILDHOOD, BOYHOOD, YOUTH

THE COSSACKS, THE DEATH OF IVAN ILYICH,
HAPPY EVER AFTER

THE PENGUIN CLASSICS

THE MOST RECENT VOLUMES

LIVY
The War with Hannibal · *Betty Radice*

BALZAC
Cousin Bette · *M. A. Crawford*

MAUPASSANT
A Woman's Life · *H. N. P. Sloman*

CLASSICAL LITERARY CRITICISM
T. S. Dorsch

PLAUTUS
The Pot of Gold and Other Plays · *E. F. Watling*

TERENCE
The Brothers and Other Plays · *Betty Radice*

PLUTARCH
Makers of Rome · *Ian Scott-Kilvert*

POEMS OF THE LATE T'ANG
A. C. Graham

PETRONIUS
The Satyricon · *J. P. Sullivan*

THE UPANISHADS
Juan Mascaró

For a complete list of books available please write to Penguin Books whose address can be found on the back of the title page